A FRIEND
of GOD

A FRIEND
of GOD

Through Sorrow and Grief
Joy and Laughter

KATIE LOPEZ

DEBARIM PUBLISHING

Debarim Publishing
807 W Broadway St.
Spiro, OK 74959
www.debarimpublishing.com

Due to the changing nature of the Internet, if there are any web
addresses, links, or URLs included in this manuscript, these may have
been altered and may no longer be accessible. The views and opinions
shared in this book belong solely to the author and do not necessarily
reflect those of the publisher. The publisher therefore disclaims
responsibility for the views or opinions expressed within the work.

Paperback ISBN-13: 979-8-9924767-2-9
Ebook ISBN-13: 979-8-9924767-3-6

Introduction

What does being a friend of God really mean? What does it look like? In Exodus 33:7–11, we see Moses talking with God in the tent of meeting, face to face, as one speaks to a friend. Later in Numbers 12:3, we see Moses was called the most humble (meek or afflicted) man on all the earth. Although a friend of God, Moses' life was full of many tests and trials. At his birth, Pharaoh tried to take Moses' life along with many other precious babies.

Later in Moses' life, he encountered many afflictions from Pharaoh and numerous challenges with the children of Israel in the desert. Through all these tests and trials, the Bible says Moses was God's friend (Exodus 33:11). He wasn't perfect, but he poured out his life for God, and God loved him as a friend. When Moses made mistakes, he repented and kept the friendship and love between him and God strong.

I do not pretend to be a Moses, but I do believe the Lord and I are good friends. It wasn't always like this though. Over the years, I have grown in my walk with the Lord immensely. I have learned one of the key points of being a friend of God seems to be many tests and trials. As my family and I have drawn closer to the Lord over the years, we've encountered both. When we messed up, we repented. When satan struck out of nowhere, we pressed into Him all the more. No matter the trial, we continue to trust and obey God, creating a very intimate friendship between us.

Over the years, the Lord has been my rock. Through the tears and sorrow, He has been and still is my comfort and my song. He, also, bountifully blessed us in ways I could never have imagined, such touches from heaven that took my breath away, such love. No matter what you're going through today, I hope you press into the Father. He is the best, most trustworthy friend you will ever have.

In Sweet Memory of

John Lopez (July 17, 2019)

Esther Lopez (December 10, 2020)

Joshua Lopez (May 16, 2021)

Gracie Lopez (May 16, 2021)

James Lopez (August 18, 2022)

Papa and Momma love you with all of our hearts
and will see you in heaven someday.

Dedication

I dedicate this book to my Father in Heaven, who made me
everything I am today.
It is by His grace this book is in your hands.
I pray it blesses and encourages you.

Table of Contents

Chapter 1

My Love for Children

Although now in my forties, I guess my desire to have children and a big family started a long time ago. I remember playing *Life*, the board game, with my neighborhood girlfriend down the street. She and I always wanted to land on the "It's a girl!" or "It's a boy!" spaces. So much so, I remember writing additional spots on the board so the chances of babies increased. We both enjoyed filling our little play cars with lots of babies.

My parents both love Jesus very much and brought me up to love Him too. I asked Jesus to be my Lord and Savior early in life, and enjoyed reading the Bible and learning about who God was. My devotion time with Him was very important to me, even as a teen and a young adult.

In my late twenties, the Lord brought my sweet husband to me. Coming right out of the Marine Corps, Sam was a little rough around the edges. Over the years, the Lord has helped us grow together and grow in Him. He is a wonderful man and loves Jesus with all his heart. He's a lot of fun, and loves people deeply. His giving heart has matured me in ways I really needed to grow. I love him dearly.

About two years after we were married, we welcomed our first child into the world, Zachariah William Lopez. It was an intense labor and delivery, but what a beautiful baby boy. He has such a gentle spirit and is very outgoing and strong-willed. He gives me a run for my money. About two years after that, we had our daughter, Taylor Anne Lopez. She is a gem with a beautiful voice. She loves Jesus with all her heart.

I was thrilled to be a mom of two now and very busy. At this point in our marriage, Sam and I loved the Lord, but we were still growing in maturity with God and one another. We were not aware of much of the supernatural side of things like angels, demons, miracles, healing, speaking in tongues, and so on. I'm ashamed to say that we were pretty much ankle or knee-deep in our relationship with Jesus. Here is what I mean by ankle or knee-deep:

> And when the man went out to the east with the line in his hand, he measured one thousand cubits, and he brought me through the waters; the water came up to my ankles. Again he measured one thousand and brought me through the waters; the water came up to my knees. Again he measured one thousand and brought me through; the water came up to my waist. Again he measured one thousand, and it was a river that I could not cross; for the water was too deep, water in which one must swim, a river that could not be crossed (Ezekiel 47:3–5).

I have found that your level of intimacy or friendship with God can directly relate to the level and size of the tests and trials you are facing.

I believe Ezekiel was shown the above levels of water as a picture of various levels of intimacy or maturity in Christ. Why am I saying all this about levels? I have found that your level of intimacy or friendship with God can directly relate to the level and size of the tests and trials you are facing.

At times, the Lord will call us into deeper waters or deeper intimacy with Him. He usually does this through tests; you can see God doing this in Deuteronomy 8:2. He tests us to see what is in our hearts, whether we will obey His commands or not. Other times, satan may throw trials at us, especially if we are threatening to him. Jesus does warn us that we will have trials and tribulations in this world. The enemy is always prowling. We must remain vigilant (John 16:33; 1 Peter 5:8).

Deeper with Jesus

As Zachariah became a young toddler, our real parenting had begun. It was important to us to explain right away to the children who God, Jesus, and the Holy Spirit were. We wanted to raise our children according to the love and guidance God shows us in His Word. We were honest with the children about Santa Clause, the Easter Bunny, and the Tooth Fairy right from the beginning. We told them *we* gave them the gifts, egg baskets, and money for lost teeth. We noticed right away this was not common, and it separated us from the parenting norm. We didn't mind though. Establishing God's truth in our home was very important to us.

As I healed from giving birth to Taylor, I began to feel off, not quite myself. My thoughts seemed slow, and words were sometimes hard to find. Migraines began, and so did depressive thoughts, followed by cold hands, cold feet, and much exhaustion. My OB ran some blood work and diagnosed me with hypothyroidism. I'm sure some of you can relate. It's not a fun disease. The doctor said it often comes after bearing children, as the thyroid works overtime to create a baby. The medication she prescribed helped, but since it was synthetic, it didn't fix the problem. It actually created more side effects. With how I was feeling, it was challenging to still nurse at night and be a fun, capable mom and wife during the day. I kept trusting the Lord and got used to a new but difficult normal.

As we continued raising the children, the Lord guided me to serve now and then in the children's ministry at church; I loved it! I found that one of the gifts the Lord had given me was teaching (Romans 12:7). The Lord also helped me shed the last few pounds from Taylor's pregnancy by joining an intense mommy-workout group. However, after joining the group, I began experiencing strange nausea and started having bathroom issues as well. It wasn't pregnancy nausea; I could tell the difference. This was different and odd. It lasted for months and months.

Finally, during a regular checkup, the ob-gyn found a cyst on my right ovary. I was hoping this was the cause of the strange symptoms. He wanted to operate but warned me I may lose my right ovary during the surgery. He would try to save it, but there was a chance I could lose it. This was very hard news to receive because Sam and I didn't feel we were finished having children. You can still have babies with one ovary, of course, but it just may take longer to conceive. Because the doctor felt it would be wise to remove the cyst, the family and I covered the procedure in prayer.

The doctor was able to remove the cyst *and* save my ovary. We were very grateful to the Lord and gave Him the glory. At this point, I thought things would calm down in our lives, but the nausea and bathroom issues persisted. Then several months later, Sam lost his position at work for what seemed to be no fault of his own.

Side Note: I have noticed the devil enjoys hitting believers in Christ back-to-back (two or more things usually within a year or less). Just a heads up—keep your armor on (Ephesians 6). He thinks this will knock the wind out of us. Don't let it. Lean into Jesus. Remember how much God loves you. Quote Scripture over yourself if you have to.

Chapter 2

Instability and Lots of Change

B ecause I stay home with the kids, Sam is the sole provider. We agreed on me staying home with the kids even before we were married. It's something we both value. Because of this, we leaned heavily on the Lord for guidance in our next steps. We loved where we lived, and did not want to move because we had a lot of friends and family near by.

Sam's job experience was in air traffic control, and he wanted to stay in his field. I didn't blame him at all. It just made things challenging. Because the FAA is a government agency, we were allowed to transfer within the agency. They gave us a list of cities and facilities we could choose from, and we were given a deadline to make our decision. None were close to where we lived. We prayed about it, and did our research the best we could. Sam really wanted to stay on the west coast, so we chose Washington (Seattle Center). We were currently living in Southern California at the time, and we knew this would be a drastic change for all of us. By faith we took the position, leaving family and friends behind.

Our Move to Washington

At this point, although extremely grateful for income, I felt very alone: no friends, a cold and wet new state to navigate, and two young children.

I was reaching an emotional breaking point. In addition, for months, I had been asking the Lord for another baby, hoping Sam would be ready. Our apartment in San Diego was so small, and things were expensive in California. Then my surgery happened, and then the job loss. Life was just not going the way I thought it should. I cried out to the Lord, and He graciously heard me.

As we settled into the home in Washington, I remember Sam commenting on how big the house was and mentioning how much easier it was to raise the kids with a little bit of land. Things weren't as expensive in Washington either. Long story short, Sam's heart opened up for more children.

About a year later, the Lord blessed us with our third child, Julia Rose Lopez. She is so precious and such a comedian! She's always making us laugh. My hope was restored. Although the temperatures were chilly and the rain kept physically falling, my heart was warm and full of joy. My Jesus saw me and gave me the desires of my heart, another baby.

> *Delight yourself also in the LORD, and He shall give you*
> *the desires of your heart* (Psalm 37:4).

At that point, I was busier than ever as I also began homeschooling Zachariah at the time. We were slowly making some friends, and I was finding my way with volunteering at our new church and hosting families for dinner or ladies for coffee. I felt like we were physically and spiritually gaining momentum for the Lord.

However, pretty soon, the rainy season started taking a toll on me. It was about eight months long each year. We lived near Seattle, and although the rain was not intense, it was usually daily or all day. If it wasn't raining, it was cloudy. Most of the time, it was about thirty-seven to forty-three degrees. It was not cold enough for snow, but not warm enough to enjoy either. In addition, because Washington was so far north on the earth's hemisphere, we were only getting eight hours of daylight at times. This made for very long nights, and we began to regret our choice of Washington. During our research before the move, we read things like annual temperatures and annual rainfall, but living it was a completely different thing.

It felt like a heaviness I couldn't see (depression) was trying to grip me. In addition, the doctor diagnosed my thyroid as getting worse after Julia's delivery and increased the medication. This caused even more discomfort. Through research online, the Lord helped me realize my liver was being taxed from the hypothyroidism. In addition, He showed me that the intense physical workouts I had grown accustom to in San Diego and was still participating in with a mom group in Washington, were causing the constant dull nausea and bathroom issues from added stress to my already compromised system. I began trying many holistic ways to heal my liver and thyroid: teas, herbs, even animal thyroid supplements because they were not synthetic. Nothing really seemed to work. Certain things helped, but not much. At this point, I was on a very high dosage of synthetic thyroid medication because the doctor said my thyroid was almost dead. Feeling depressed on top of all this was incredibly challenging.

Sam tried everything he could to help me. He gave me a tanning membership for vitamin D because the sun was hardly out. He bought me a special lamp for my thyroid, which I tried to sit under daily for an hour or so. He also changed almost all the lights in the house to be a natural day light tone. It all helped, but wasn't enough. The physical and mental rain kept pouring down on me. We kept trusting the Lord, crying out to Him for guidance, and waiting on Him for direction.

Sam's work in Seattle Center was going well, but he felt God leading him to apply for a transfer within the FAA back down to Southern California. We were hoping and praying he would get picked up so we could transfer back to our friends, family, and the sunshine. Beyond all odds, Sam got picked up at a facility about three hours from where we used to live in Southern California. We were elated and took the transfer immediately. Once I was back in the sunshine, I felt much better mentally. My thyroid and liver were still not whole, but the depression was gone almost immediately. Thank you, Jesus.

Side Note: I believe depression is actually a demon. If left unchecked (if you don't rebuke it as a demon in Jesus' name), it can actually hold on long enough to create physical symptoms and blood work to prove itself. I believe it masks itself as a disease. Then folks unknowingly start saying they have depression, which further allows it to stay. Our words are very powerful. "Death and life are in the power of the tongue, and those who love it will eat its fruit" (Proverbs 18:21).

I didn't want to play around with depression, as I could feel how strong it was near Seattle. I was trusting the Lord, and I'm sure I rebuked it in Jesus' name as a demon, but I also knew that living where the sun would shine more often would help, and it did.

Side Note: If you are struggling with depression, repent to the Lord of being depressed. Then rebuke depression in Jesus' name. Keep trusting the Lord and singing His praise. Ask God for wisdom, and move away from whatever may be depressing you if possible (city, people, weather). Sometimes it's just a regional spirit in the area or with the person or city. In our case, it was regional. It did not follow us; it seems to be imbedded in Seattle (Mark 5:10 talks about demons not wanting to leave their region).

Here are some Bible verses about sickness and oppression being linked to demons or satan.

> *When evening had come, they brought to Him many who were demon-possessed. And He cast out the spirits with a word, and healed all who were sick, that it might be fulfilled which was spoken by Isaiah the prophet, saying: "He Himself took our infirmities and bore our sicknesses"* (Matthew 8:16–17).

> *How God anointed Jesus of Nazareth with the Holy Spirit and with power, who went about doing good and healing all who were oppressed by the devil, for God was with Him* (Acts 10:38).

> *And He came down with them and stood on a level place with a crowd of His disciples and a great multitude of people from all Judea and Jerusalem, and from the seacoast of Tyre and Sidon, who came to hear Him and be healed of their diseases, as well as those who were tormented with unclean spirits* (Luke 6:17–18).

Our Move (Back) to California

We were very happy to return to California where we were blessed with mostly sunny skies. We found a church right away, and both Sam and I got busy serving. I kept studying the Scriptures faithfully and growing in my walk with the Lord.

One of the things I hadn't quite understood yet was how to receive healing from Jesus. I became very hungry for it though as the synthetic pharmacy medication was hard on my system. Although the herbs and teas were not healing my thyroid or liver, I saw in Scripture that Jesus could heal both. How could I receive this healing? Does Jesus still heal today? Various believers and churches seemed to have mixed opinions about God healing today. Why?

> *Side Note: One of satan's biggest tactics is to cloak himself. He enjoys hiding behind things like names of diseases. If we think it's just hypothyroidism, depression, alcoholism, lower back pain, we won't think in terms of spiritual warfare. We won't think to rebuke it like a demon or lay hands on it for healing (2 Corinthians 11:14) (John 8:44).*

Miraculous Healing

The Lord had such a surprise in store for me. A couple of days after the new thyroid doctor in California increased the dosage of my medication (yet again), I was very discouraged. That afternoon I joined a FaceTime prayer call. My sister, mother, and a couple of women from Michigan and I were all meeting to pray together. We were meeting to specifically pray for my sister, Sally.

Before we opened the prayer time, Sally asked if anyone had other prayer requests. When it was my turn, I mentioned my thyroid. I believed God could heal me, but my faith was small. I threw it out there anyway. Jesus Christ is the same yesterday, today, and forever, right (Hebrews 13:8)? If He could heal back then, well, how about now?

Another gal asked for prayer for her sinuses, and then we began to pray. We covered Sally in prayer for her request first, but then we began to cover the "add-on" prayer requests. Earlier, I had prayed over some olive oil, and put it on my neck. As my mother started praying for my thyroid, I put my hand on my neck, and I began to feel a warm sensation all over it. For those of you who may not know, the thyroid is a butterfly-shaped organ on both sides of your neck. It began to pop and sizzle! What was going on? I was astounded! Holy Spirit immediately let me know God was healing my thyroid right then! I cried out, "Ladies, keep praying; my throat is crackling and popping over here!" One or two of the ladies broke into praying in tongues, and the rest kept praying in English.

My thyroid remained warm and kept popping on and off for about ten minutes. I believe the popping was the Lord healing the nodules that had developed on my thyroid gland. He was bringing the blood flow back. What the doctor called almost dead, the Lord was raising to life! Hallelujah.

In my spirit, I kept hearing, "I love you, Katie. I love you, Katie. I love you." I couldn't stop smiling! I also felt a good tingling in my head later that afternoon. It felt like my brain was receiving signals or something it needed. The Lord had miraculously healed my thyroid. In addition, the woman who needed sinus healing said she received healing too. She said her sinuses were draining and opening up as we prayed. Thank you, Jesus, for being our healer!

After speaking with the Lord, He guided me off all herbal remedies. He confirmed that He had healed my thyroid, and it would take some time for my liver and other organs to align, but that I should go off my synthetic thyroid medication immediately. I obeyed.

To this day, I am doing great and off all medication. When Jesus heals, He locks things up tight. The doctor agreed that I had experienced a miraculous healing. My blood work reflected it. In addition, the constant dull nausea and bathroom issues went away as my liver was restored over time. The Lord brought me to complete wholeness. I will thank Him forever.

Side Note: The Lord truly loves all of us. When Jesus was on earth, the Bible says He went around doing good and healing all those oppressed by the devil (Acts 10:38). The devil was oppressing me with hypothyroidism, and Jesus healed me! He is the same yesterday, today, and forever (Hebrews 13:8). Please believe Jesus for your healing as well. Jesus still heals today! I am proof.

Here are some healing verses to encourage you.

And these signs will follow those who believe: In My name they will cast out demons; they will speak with new tongues; they will take up serpents; and if they drink anything deadly, it will by no means hurt them; they will lay hands on the sick, and they will recover (Mark 16:17–18).

Is anyone among you sick? Let him call for the elders of the church, and let them pray over him, anointing him with oil in the name of the Lord. And the prayer of faith will save the sick, and the Lord will raise him up. And if he has committed sins, he will be forgiven. Confess your trespasses to one another, and pray for one another, that you may be healed. The effective, fervent prayer of a righteous man avails much (James 5:14–16).

Chapter 3

Angel Visitation and the Separation

T here was already a hunger for Jesus in my heart, but after this miraculous healing, there was a distinct shift in our family to believe God for more. We began to take God at His Word. We had experiential knowledge of His goodness in a *huge way* now, and there was no going back.

One evening a couple of months later, my son Zachariah (about seven at the time) raced into my room, telling me there was an angel in his bedroom! I knew Zach could see in the Spirit, so I was very excited. The passage in 1 Samuel 3 came to my mind. It's where a similar thing happened when little Samuel came to Eli, the priest. Eli told Samuel to go back to his room and stay there to hear from the Lord. With this passage on my mind, I told Zach, "Please go back to your room, and wait there. Listen to whatever the angel tells you." I very excitedly waited in the other room, wondering what an angel was saying to my son.

Zachariah came out a bit later, telling me everything he could remember. He said the angel was *huge*. That it was inside and outside his room all at the same time somehow. It was taller than the house, but somehow in the house still. He also said the angel was *very* bright, so bright he could hardly look at him. He mentioned the angel being a bright golden color. He said his wings came down to a V-shape with feathers on the very tips of them. He said the angel smiled, waved, and then began to speak. Zach said that when the angel waved, he wasn't as afraid and was able to listen to what he said. He couldn't remember all of it, but I'll never forget this part. Zachariah said the angel told him, "Keep your robes white."

Since that visitation, and looking back to Zachariah's difficult birth, I can see that the enemy has had eyes on him for a while. The nurse told me at the time of Zach's birth that she'd been a labor and delivery nurse for over twenty years. She said something like, "Honey, everything that could go wrong in labor and delivery went wrong for you." She called his birth a perfect storm. She said it was the worst labor and delivery she'd ever seen. I thought it was rough, but it was my first child. I had nothing to compare it with. I'll spare you the details, but they used about everything you could use to help deliver a child. It was long and intense.

At one point, Zachariah's heart beat dropped, and the doctor was about to perform an emergency C-section. One more push, though, and he was out and began to breathe normally. All that to say, I believe Zach has a special calling on his life because of the warfare I saw at his birth and now this angel visitation.

Sam and I pray often for Zach as we can see a tug-of-war within him at times. It's a light vs. darkness that we do not see in the other children. Over the years, I have seen light always win in the end. Praise God. At times, seeing these struggles I wonder if that's why the Lord sent an angel, simply to encourage Zachariah. My husband and I are very diligent in reminding Zach to keep his robes white. We are very thankful for the visitation, and blessed to have Zachariah in our lives.

The Separation

The love and power of Jesus was really coming alive for us. I never doubted God's love for us, but this new personal side of Jesus was amazing! I couldn't stop smiling and telling everyone about my healing and about the angel. I wanted to share God's love and this personal side of Him with everyone. My God was big enough to love and meet everyone's needs, to heal everyone and set them free. The sky was the limit!

As I continued to study the Word of God, I began to have more prophetic dreams; the Lord opened my ears spiritually, and I began to hear in the Spirit often. Hearing in the Spirit is hearing things that happen in the other realm, not the physical realm/world. I began to hear both good and bad (a gate opening, a door shutting, a shofar sounding, demons speaking, God and angels speaking, and other things). I also began understanding harder concepts in the Bible. Sam and the kids were growing in the Lord as well.

We were finally beginning to mature in Christ; eating steak (harder concepts in the Word of God), not milk (easier concepts). When I would mention this steak to friends at church like laying hands for healing, casting out the demons in Jesus' name, or speaking in tongues and being filled with the Holy Spirit power like Jesus intended for all believers, I was surprised it was not received well. People were skeptical. They were happy I was healed, but not sure about rebuking demons in Jesus' name or laying hands for healing. There was a definite hard pass about speaking in tongues. It seemed foreign to them or even controversial. *Why*, I wondered.

Looking back, it wasn't just our church body. Most churches we'd gone to over the years were the same. They'd gotten into the routine of two to three services Sunday morning, get-'em-in/ get-'em-out. Rush, rush, rush. Only the greeters really said hello. Three songs, smoke machines, lights, and so on. Someone would give a ten-minute teaching on tithes, and the pastor would give a twenty-minute sermon snack with funny stories. One more short song, and have a great week. Halfway through Monday afternoon, who really remembered what was preached the day before?

I realized there was no real power coming from the gospel being preached at most churches. People were still really struggling in their lives with physical ailments, financial strain, demonic strongholds, and the list goes on. No one at church was getting healed to speak of or talking about supernatural experiences. People didn't seem to be changed or set free. I began to realize the church body (by and large) had simply lost her way; she'd lost most of her salt and light. It wasn't about loving people and preaching the full gospel anymore. The controversial, potent Scriptures that could really set people free were being left out of most sermons because they were offensive and might lose numbers (and tithe checks).

Somehow it wasn't about loving people anymore and meeting their needs. It had become corporate, and about money. Folks were still hurting and broken, but I saw that they weren't being taught and loved by the church at the level Jesus intended. Since the full gospel message wasn't being preached (by most churches), neither was the power of the Holy Spirit to bring change with signs and wonders following. All that to say, I think that is why these friends were so skeptical about healings, deliverance, and tongues; these topics weren't really being preached. In fact, some churches were even preaching against them.

For our gospel did not come to you in word only, but also in power, and in the Holy Spirit and in much assurance, as you know what kind of men we were among you for your sake (1 Thessalonians 1:5).

And my speech and my preaching were not with persuasive words of human wisdom, but in demonstration of the Spirit and of power, that your faith should not be in the wisdom of men but in the power of God (1 Corinthians 2:4–5).

Our family was experiencing the deep love of God and the life-changing power of the Holy Spirit, but it wasn't coming from church. It was coming from our friendship and intimacy with God – at home. I believe the Lord was gracious to our family because of our hunger for Him. We had been diligently seeking Him and taking Him at His Word. No matter what the church was preaching, we chose to believe God's Word and obey and practice what we saw in Scripture, no matter how hard the concept. We would often share these truths with others (preaching the gospel – even hard verses). I believe this kind of faith and trust in Jesus opened the doors for the Holy Spirit power to start flowing in our lives with miracles, signs, and wonders.

But without faith it is impossible to please Him, for he who comes to God must believe that He is, and that He is a rewarder of those who diligently seek Him (Hebrews 11:6).

So then, after the Lord had spoken to them, He was received up into heaven, and sat down at the right hand of God. And they went out and preached everywhere, the

Lord working with them and confirming the word through
the accompanying signs. Amen (Mark 16:19–20).

> **Signs and wonders are to follow the preaching of the gospel. If there are no signs and wonders, then what kind of gospel is being preached?**

It is God's will for the entire church (all believers) to seek Him and to grow into maturity and unity of the faith. He desires all of us to love Him, to love others, and to preach God's Word wherever we go. As we do this, signs and wonders will follow us to confirm God's Word (Mark 16:20; Ephesians 4:7–16; John 17:20–26). Bottom line: Signs and wonders are to follow the preaching of the gospel. If there are no signs and wonders, then what kind of gospel is being preached?

Needless to say, the shift in friendships and awkwardness began. Wherever we went, my family and I would do our best to follow Holy Spirit's prompting. We would lay hands on the sick and believe God to heal. We would rebuke demons in Jesus' name and expect them to go. The children and I would sing and sing at home and wait on the Lord. We wouldn't rush our worship to Him. We would pray and sing in English, and then we would pray and sing in tongues as the apostle Paul instructs us to (1 Corinthians 14:15). At church or when folks would come over to the house for dinner or a play date, we'd excitedly tell them what God was doing in our lives. We kept encouraging them to believe God for more, to really get to know God and love Him on a deeper level.

Chapter 4

Baby John and Snowflakes from Heaven

Over the years, I've grown to realize that supernatural healings and visitations usually flag the attention of satan. Although I love it when God shows up with signs and wonders, they seem to put an "x" on your spiritual forehead by the enemy. Not an issue; we believers just need to keep our guard up. Back then I was not quite aware of all this yet.

It was early spring of 2019, and my heart was ready for another baby. I could sense we were still not done having children and began praying for another baby. The Lord answered quickly, and baby number four was on the way. It was a typical first-trimester pregnancy for the most part. Nausea and tiredness set in fairly quickly. I say "for the most part" because the Lord was trying to warn my husband and me about the enemy's attempts against this baby. We both started having odd thoughts and dreams about the baby not living and of being physically hurt in some way.

Back then, I didn't realize God was sending us warning dreams. Sam didn't realize it either, so we both just kept hoping the dreams would not come to pass. Since I was very busy in that season of our lives (helping with VBS, studying for my realtor's license, and serving in the homeschool co-op), unfortunately, I didn't lean into the Holy Spirit for guidance about these thoughts and dreams.

It wasn't until week twelve that I was able to see the ob-gyn for the first baby appointment. Sam was working that day, so I loaded all the kiddos into the van, and we took off. As the children filed into the low-lit exam room and sat down, I climbed up onto the exam chair. The ultrasound gal was preparing my tummy with cream to look at the baby on the monitor. As the tech began, I waited excitedly to hear the baby's heartbeat for the first time. I pointed out to the children the baby on the monitor. They were all smiles. The tech quietly said to me, "You may want to hold off speaking to your children about the baby just yet Ma'am . . . I don't see any cardiac movement."

I looked back at the screen . . . dazed. *What did she just say?* Stunned. I knew cardiac meant heart, and I was trying to process everything as quickly as I could. I could see the child in my womb on the monitor. His head, his body, everything . . . He looked perfect! But she was right. I finally realized there was no movement. None. The babe wasn't moving at all, and his heart wasn't beating either. I sat there stunned.

She took some quick measurements of the baby and then explained that although I thought I was week twelve and five days, the baby was only measuring week twelve and one day. She said, "Everything looks beautiful: the baby, your waters, the sac, the umbilical cord. He must have passed away about four days ago, Ma'am. I have no idea why this happened. I am so sorry, Ma'am."

My logical side kicked in for a minute, quickly remembering my nausea and breast tenderness fading about three to four days prior and quite abruptly at that, but again being so busy, I had just chalked it up to me coming out of the first trimester and going into the second. Nausea during pregnancy naturally fades about then anyway. Then my emotional side took over. I was still in shock as she cleaned up the cream on my tummy.

I slowly stood up, and Zachariah (about eight years old then) thoughtfully asked, "What's wrong, Momma? Is the baby ok?"

I felt the hot sting of tears coming to my eyes as I blinked back quickly and choked out, "The . . . the baby is in heaven, Honey. He didn't make it."

The tech quickly whisked us into another room to consult with the doctor. The doctor explained that this was not my fault, and this happens sometimes. I was barely listening. The tears just wouldn't stop, and I began to sob violently. Looking back, I believe I was going into shock. I remember holding onto Zachariah's hand so tightly as he sat next to me in the room. The doctor came and went, trying to schedule things for a second ultrasound and also schedule a D&C; everything was happening so quickly. Zachariah looked at me and said, "Momma, I can see Jesus with the baby right now. He is holding the baby. It's ok, Momma. The baby is with Jesus."

As I mentioned earlier, Zach can see in the Spirit. He often sees things in heaven, but he can also see angels and demons here on earth. In those moments, my spirit was *very* comforted; I knew for certain God placed Zachariah in the room with me that day to encourage me. I held tightly to his hand and tried to smile. I remember thanking him for being so strong for me that day.

Dreams from Jesus

Before I share what happened next, I'd like to take some time and talk about dreams from Jesus. During those first precious weeks of pregnancy with baby number four, spiritual warfare over the child's life had begun, but I didn't realize it.

The Lord seemed to be warning me with dream after dream that something was up – they were dreams regarding the baby not living or leaving my womb early. Come to find out, Sam had similar dreams or thoughts as well. He just wasn't sure why or what to do about it either. I believe satan was also at work, throwing some arrows of fear and doubt into my heart. That spring my cousin lost her baby girl about half way through the pregnancy. I felt so badly for her and prayed for her. I noticed this planted a seed of fear in my heart, hoping I wouldn't lose my baby during pregnancy as well. Then, during the same timeframe, the kids and I were enjoying *Little House on the Prairie*, Season 1. One episode was hard though – Carylon gave birth to her fourth child, but then lost him quickly to a blood disease. Again, another seed of fear was planted.

I believe Jesus was warning us of satan's plan through these dreams and hoping we would do something about it. In Ephesians 6, the apostle Paul tells us to keep our shield of faith up against the fiery darts of the enemy. I believe satan was shooting arrows of fear and death at us. I'm not sure what caused the baby's death, but I do believe it was satan in some way, whether in the form of chromosomes not working together (like the doctor said) or some other kind of sickness. The Bible does say that satan takes life.

> *The thief does not come except to steal, and to kill, and to destroy. I have come that they may have life, and that they may have it more abundantly* (John 10:10).

Looking back at all the supernatural help we were receiving at the time, I believe satan was beginning to see our family as a threat. We were encouraging others to believe that God was good, and that He could heal them and set them free. I could be wrong, but I believe satan was trying to throw us off course with the miscarriage. I believe he was hoping we'd give up on God when the baby didn't live, or at least that we would shut our mouths about how good God was.

The bottom line is that Jesus gave us warning dreams that we did nothing about. In addition, I had fear and didn't repent of it. To be clear, over the years, I have learned that the world is *not* cut and dry; even when we do everything right, things can still go wrong. Jesus Himself warns us of trouble in this world (John 16:33). What I'm saying is once we received the warning dreams, at least we should have taken authority over the devil and his schemes commanding what we saw in the dreams not to happen in Jesus' name. At least we should have repented of fear. We co-labor with God.

> *Behold, I give you the authority to trample on serpents and scorpions, and over all the power of the enemy, and nothing shall by any means hurt you* (Luke 10:19).

> *For God has not given us a spirit of fear, but of power and of love and of a sound mind* (2 Timothy 1:7).

> *For we are God's fellow workers; you are God's field, you are God's building* (1 Corinthians 3:9).

Not that everything would have turned out in our favor, but at least we could have done our part. We were still learning about spiritual warfare back then.

Side Note: If you receive a warning dream from Jesus, don't wait. Sit up right then and take authority over it in Jesus' name. If you are a believer in Jesus, know that He has given you authority to come against the plans of the enemy.

> *Behold, I give you the authority to trample on serpents and scorpions, and over all the power of the enemy, and nothing shall by any means hurt you* (Luke 10:19).

> *Assuredly, I say to you, whatever you bind on earth will be bound in heaven, and whatever you loose on earth will be loosed in heaven* (Matthew 8:18).

Side Note: If you are aware of any sin in your life, like I was with some fear about the baby not making it, repent. Unconfessed sin leaves doors open that satan can use against you. It allows him to call in your harvest (you reap what you sow; Galatians 6:7). Instead, let's be like Jesus; He had no sin for satan to use against Him.

> *I will no longer talk much with you, for the ruler of this world is coming, and he has nothing in Me* (John 14:30).

> *So submit to [the authority of] God. Resist the devil [stand firm against him] and he will flee from you* (James 4:7 AMP).

Now that we know what warning dreams are, we've stopped many attempts by satan against our family by simply commanding the bad things we saw in the dream not to happen in Jesus' name and praying against them. If you have a bad dream about something to come in the future about yourself or someone else, that's what I call a warning dream. Ask Holy Spirit if there is anything specific to say, but normally I just command anything I have seen in the warning dream not to happen in Jesus' name. I bind the devil and break his power in Jesus' name. Then I loose angels to help make the situation right, and make sure the bad thing I saw in the dream doesn't happen in Jesus' name. I also like to declare the opposite of what I saw in the dream. I speak good things over the person or situation. If I saw death, I declare long life. If I saw sickness, I declare health, and so on.

> *Assuredly, I say to you, whatever you bind on earth will be bound in heaven, and whatever you loose on earth will be loosed in heaven* (Matthew 18:18).

> *You will also declare a thing, and it will be established for you; so light will shine on your ways* (Job 22:28).

The opposite is also true. I have found that if you have a blessing dream from Jesus, you should agree with it by faith and talk about it like it's already done. These are wonderful or exciting dreams, something amazing that you almost can't believe, something good in your future. You'll see later where we pull in blessing dreams Jesus gave us by agreeing with God in our hearts and saying the good things we saw in the dream out loud by faith.

Now faith is the substance of things hoped for, the evidence of things not seen. For by it the elders obtained a good testimony (Hebrews 11:1).

Prayer for Resurrection from the Dead

Although the doctor highly recommended a D&C, we didn't feel like that was right for us. No signs of infection had set in; I felt fine enough to wait. It's what they call a missed miscarriage because I wasn't bleeding yet. My body hadn't let go yet.

I remember struggling to wrap my head around what happened. Did God do this to us? Did satan do this? Was this our own fault? There were so many questions. I didn't know about John 10:10 yet, so I began asking Jesus for answers. A few strong women of God met with me to pray. As we talked, they reminded me that satan is often the one who takes life.

The thief does not come except to steal, and to kill, and to destroy. I have come that they may have life, and that they may have it more abundantly (John 10:10).

Knowing this was very comforting. Still showing no sign of miscarriage, I asked the ladies if they would pray with me for resurrection from the dead for this baby, so his heart would start beating again. They agreed and laid hands on my tummy and prayed with me for the child's heart to beat again. He commands us believers to raise the dead; why not start now? If He still heals today, then He still raises the dead today too.

And as you go, preach, saying, "The kingdom of heaven is at hand." Heal the sick, cleanse the lepers, raise the dead, cast out demons. Freely you have received, freely give (Matthew 10:7–8).

Nothing seemed to happen that day, but we kept praying and believing God to raise the baby to life and heal him of anything. My faith expected God to do this and for the baby to continue to grow in my womb normally. When other believers in Christ asked how I was doing, I'd explain the situation, that we were praying for resurrection from the dead for the baby, and the awkward separation continued.

I thought encouraging them to believe for healing was tough, but encouraging them to pray for resurrection from the dead was much harder. Most were just used to seeing things in the natural realm and were concerned for my health. I appreciated their love for me, but what I really wanted was for them to believe with me for a miracle. There were a few precious souls who believed and were praying persistently with us for the baby to come back.

To encourage my faith, I began to read all the Scriptures in the Bible where Jesus or other saints had raised someone from the dead. I wasn't exactly sure how to do it or how to believe for it. It wasn't a hot topic taught at most churches, and I didn't personally know anyone who'd done it. Turning to Scripture was the only answer.

I studied passage after passage in God's Word, where someone was raised from the dead. I was chewing and meditating on every verse, trying to understand how to raise someone from the dead myself (with God's power working through me, of course). Attempting to follow their method, I would say what they said and do what they did. It was very challenging to remain in faith, especially as the days dragged on.

We had a follow-up ultrasound. Still no heartbeat. Still no bleeding. I begged God. I pleaded, I sang, I cried, I waited. I read Scripture. I prayed. I waited.

We prayed for weeks, but as time went on, my body slowly let go of the pregnancy, and I began to bleed. After a very intense demonic dream, where I sensed a demon pulling the baby's body from me, I awoke. Within hours, my water broke, and I delivered his body quietly, in tears, at home. I was far enough along to tell that he was a boy. We named him John Lopez. My spirit knows he has a quiet temperament. He loves to read, and really enjoys apples.

My dad had a dream during this time of the Father, saying, "Tell her to accept my decision." He knew the "her" was me. Finally, I emotionally let go and accepted Jesus' answer. My dad's dream from the Lord really helped me move forward.

There were many touches from Jesus during these weeks of waiting and praying. I feel like we were growing spiritually by leaps and bounds. My ears became warm often, and I started hearing in the Spirit even more. My hands became warm and tingly often, so I would lay hands on anyone in the family who so much as had a headache or a fever; I would rebuke the sickness or fever and pray for healing. One time, the fever miraculously left Zachariah about sixty seconds after I rebuked it in Jesus' name. Hallelujah! Also, my daughter Taylor had several visions of the Lion of Judah being in and around our home. We knew the Lord was ever present.

My heart was crushed when Baby John stayed in heaven, but through the process, my love for the Lord grew stronger, and our friendship has grown deeper. Little did I know this was just the beginning of our journey in the valley.

Yea, though I walk through the valley of the shadow of death, I will fear no evil; For You are with me; Your rod and Your staff, they comfort me (Psalm 23:4).

Snowflakes from Heaven

A week later or so, I went into the doctor's office for a follow-up appointment. She said there were quite a few clots, and recommended I take pills to encourage fake contractions to clean out my uterus and avoid any infection.

I remember being in so much physical pain. There is a lot of blood loss with a miscarriage. My body was exhausted, and my hormones were trying to figure everything out. Not many women talk about the physical pain of miscarriage and the nausea that follows. There is so much nausea as your body tries to right itself. Then, of course, there is the emotional pain and emptiness you feel as well.

After leaving the doctor's office and getting the prescription, I remember telling Jesus something like, "Ok Lord, I just need help getting the groceries. I'll go home, then take the medication and rest while you heal my body."

I was in so much physical pain as I stepped out of my car at the grocery store that I was limping. I slowly put one foot in front of the other. I asked the angels to help me as I leaned heavily on my shopping cart. I knew they could hear me, and I knew God would commission them to help me.

Are they not all ministering spirits sent forth to minister for those who will inherit salvation? (Hebrews 1:14)

After getting most of the items I needed, I will never *ever* forget what happened next. I remember slowing down in the hair/cosmetic aisle. I think I put some Epsom salt in the cart, thinking a warm bath would help. Then I paused, the sting of hot tears began again; I tried to quickly blink them back as I said to myself, *Maybe I should get a new hairbrush or some lotion?* I hadn't thought about myself in a long, long time. *Yes, let me look here awhile and find a new brush.*

Just then, white snowflake-like particles started floating down on top of me. I instantly looked up, thinking, *What is this?* Was someone shaking dust or something from the rafters of the grocery store? Maybe the workers were moving old boxes above me. Nothing physical was moving above me, just bare rafters of the store's roof. I looked again, and the white particles continued to fall on me. I put my hand out, and I didn't feel a thing, but the "flakes" were falling all over my hand and arm and then disappearing. I looked long range down the aisles, the "snowflakes" were not everywhere; just . . . could it be . . . over me? Yes, they were just over me, and as I moved, they moved with me! I looked at the other shoppers, and they didn't seem to see a thing. The "flakes" started about three feet above me and gently fell all around me to about my waist or so and then disappeared. I was amazed!

Weeks later as I healed, the Lord had me review my journal notes, and I found a note where He said (prior to delivering John's body), "Your dress is almost ready." At that time, I just wrote it down, although I didn't understand it. I know this is extra revelation, but I believe the Lord gave me a white dress or robe that day as the snow-like white particles fell all around me. I felt His love in such a deep way. I believe I was seeing through my spiritual eyes as no one else saw the beautiful, white "snowflakes" falling. It is a favorite memory of mine to this day.

I will greatly rejoice in the Lord, my soul shall be joyful in my God; for he has clothed me with the garments of salvation, he has covered me with the robe of righteousness, as a bridegroom decks himself with ornaments, and as a bride adorns herself with her jewels (Isaiah 61:10).

Water Baptism

As the Lord healed my body, He began healing my heart too. He had to teach me that I was still a good mother. Losing this child was not a reflection of being a bad mother. To prove His point, the Lord allowed Zachariah and Taylor to be water baptized about that time. They had already asked Jesus into their hearts a few years earlier. Seeing our children make good choices and follow Jesus publicly was *just* what I needed during this season to encourage me, and God knew it. Thank you, Jesus.

Zachariah & Taylor getting baptized in the ocean

Chapter 5

Julia Rose

I t was late September 2019 now, a few months after Baby John moved to heaven. Physically and emotionally, I was doing much better. A mother never forgets her baby or babies in heaven; you just get used to the idea that they are not with you. For me at the time, I got used to three of my children being with me on earth, and one being with Jesus in heaven.

It was a typical evening in Ventura, California, except that Sam was out of town that week on a missions trip/training in Colorado. His mom was over to help with the kids while he was away. We had just finished dinner, and the kids were playing in the backyard. Little did I know my life would change drastically in seconds. Taylor burst into the house, urgently trying to explain how Julia (two and a half years old) was not responding. "Momma, she's just staring at the sky! We keep saying her name, but she's not responding!"

I ran outside, knelt down next to Julia, and said her name several times. "Julia. Julia!" But she wasn't responding. I gently picked her up and realized she was still breathing. She wasn't responding, though; she was just staring at the sky. Then she became rigid, arching her back. Grabbing my purse, I began running with her to the van to head to the ER. I had *no* idea what was going on or if I needed to do CPR.

The Holy Spirit said, "No, she's breathing; don't do CPR." *But what was happening?* I thought. Forgetting my shoes, I yelled back to Mom-in-law as I jumped into the van, "Pray! Stay with Zach!"

It seemed like every second counted. Taylor jumped into the back seat, and we took off. I held Julia with one hand and drove with the other. It was the longest ten minutes of my life. She started to jerk again and again and again. Her eyes rolled back. I kept whispering into her ear as I drove, "I'm here, Honey. You're not alone. I'm here. I know something is wrong. We will figure it out, Baby. I love you."

Throwing the van into park at the ER entry, I yelled, "Taylor, get my purse!" She did. My adrenaline racing, I hobbled to the front door in socks (no shoes on), hoping Taylor was following me—sweet Julia still rigid in my arms. As we entered the waiting area full of people, I nervously shouted, "She's not responding, and she's having a hard time breathing!" It was like the Red Sea parting. Everyone backed out of the way and let us through to the front of the line. The staff immediately ushered us back. The doctor and nurses began taking her vitals; then all the questions began. I did my best to answer, still somewhat in panic mode. Was she hurt? Did she fall? How did this happen? I said "No, the kids were just playing in the backyard. I don't know. I have no idea what's wrong."

After a bit, her eyes started to focus on me, and she began to chew the medical cords around her and fidget with things. She still wasn't herself, but I was so thankful she was still breathing and doing something with her hands. Then she became very sleepy. They kept monitoring her and put us in another room.

About an hour later, Julia woke up and said something to Taylor, recognizing her. My heart leapt for joy! After that, I started to breathe more easily. They did a cat scan and monitored her for a couple more hours. They said they could not find anything wrong with her; she did register a tiny fever when they checked her vitals, so they thought it was just a somewhat common toddler fever-induced seizure and most likely would never happen again. They released us and sent us home. She seemed herself again. I was confused and traumatized but very thankful to be going home.

However, in early December, Julia had another fever and another episode, much less traumatic but still very noticeable. Also, during the same few weeks around this second episode, she kept "tripping" on what seemed like nothing and falling to the ground, and her head kept dropping to the table for no apparent reason. I was hoping she was banging it on purpose for some reason while playing with playdough or eating, but in my heart, I knew something was wrong.

Later that first week in December, it just let loose—all kinds of seizures and eye twitching. Julia screamed out for us; I ran to her and held her in my arms, praying and praying that the seizures would stop. We had *no* idea what was happening to our baby girl. There was no fever this time either. We took her back to the Ventura ER, where they ran a mini-EEG on her. The neurologist diagnosed her with three kinds of rare forms of epilepsy. He said, "Most children with epilepsy have only one form, but we found three in your daughter, one of which some children do not live past their teens. We are referring you to UCLA Pediatric Neurology. They deal with this more often."

Sam and I were crushed. We could hardly breathe. I tried to listen; the doctor was saying a lot of big words, and bless him, his bedside manner wasn't the best, so I tuned out as my thoughts raced. *Not our little Julia? How is this possible? Not Julia? She's so young! What is happening, Lord? This isn't how I saw our life going . . . this isn't right. Jesus, help!*

39

Side Note: I have noticed that not only does satan like to hit believers back-to-back, but he also intensifies his overall hit the stronger the believer is in Jesus. In other words, as you become a threat to satan, he brings in the big guns (the bigger demons, the bigger attacks). It's good for us to know our enemy. As believers in Jesus Christ, we must remain vigilant.

By increasing our love and obedience to Jesus and believing in resurrection from the dead, I think we were increasing our overall threat to the kingdom of darkness. I'm sure my thyroid healing and the angel visitation also flagged satan's attention. In turn, it seemed satan became frantic, intensifying strikes towards us back-to-back. First, his attack on Baby John, and now he was threatening to take Julia. satan can see how much we love children, and he was probably hoping this would stop us from loving Jesus and throw us off course. Similar spiritual warfare seemed to happen in Paul's life as well:

> *And lest I should be exalted above measure by the abundance of the revelations, a thorn in the flesh was given to me, a messenger of Satan to buffet me, lest I be exalted above measure* (2 Corinthians 12:7).

Shortly after seeing the Ventura doctor, I scheduled the EEG with UCLA, which was an overnight exam. As I got ready that morning to take Julia in, I looked into the mirror and heard in my spirit, "Would you like to go on a journey with Me?" I quickly said yes, uncertain of what it could mean but willing to trust the Lord. Later, I found out Jesus was inviting me on a special journey to receive Julia's healing.

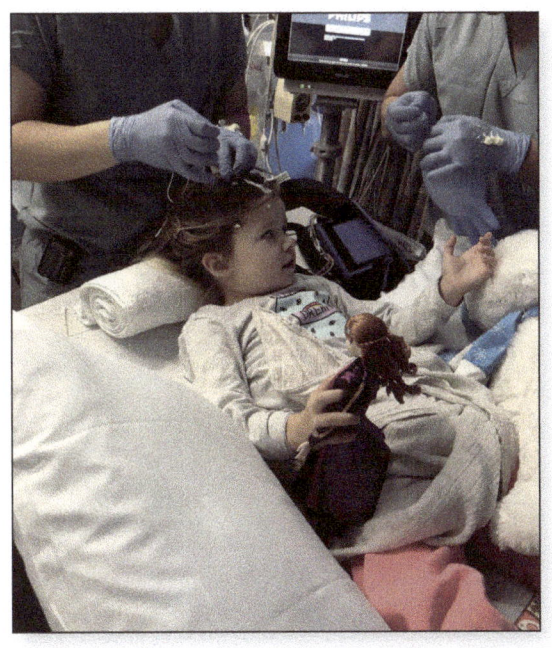

Julia (three-years-old) being hooked up to the overnight EEG machine at UCLA

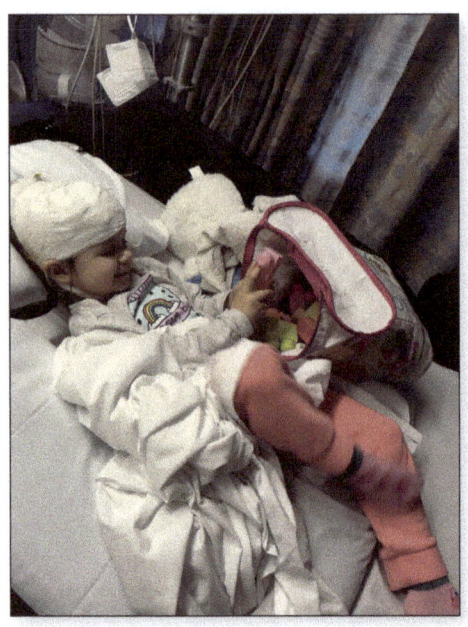

They wrapped her head so she wouldn't pull out the wires

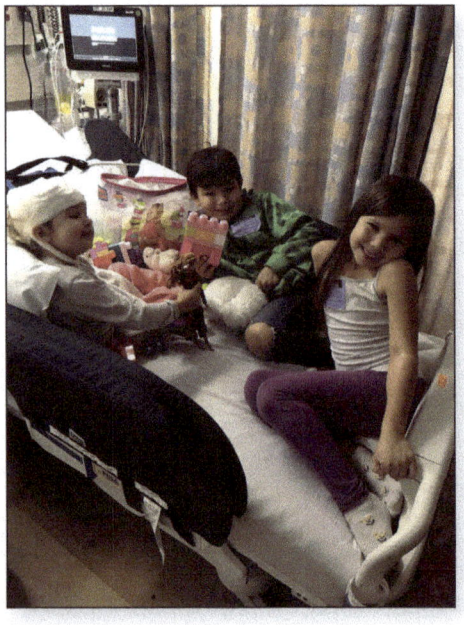

Zach and Taylor joining Julia for company

The Journey Begins

The first few weeks after the diagnosis were a blur: an overnight stay at UCLA, more doctors, lots of medication, pharmacies, tests for Julia's eyes, more appointments, blood work, tears, questions, all kinds of questions for the doctors and for Jesus. This all went down in December, so we basically skipped Christmas that year; there was no time to really enjoy it. We weren't even totally healed from losing our sweet Baby John, and now our attention turned fully to our precious Julia. My emotions were raw.

One night in December, in my meager attempt to give the kids some Christmas fun, I met up with one of my close friends, Suzanne, and her family. She loves Jesus like crazy. We were watching the Christmas light boat show by the marina. As we quietly walked along, I remember saying, "Suzanne, it seems all too familiar and back-to-back; I hate feeling helpless as satan is attacking another child of ours! First John, now Julia." She agreed.

Does Satan Give People Sickness?

Some of you may be having a hard time with thinking satan was behind John's death and Julia's diagnosis. To be clear, I do not believe satan causes all death or sickness, but at times I think he can. In our case, I think he did.

Maybe you're not sure of the connection between being a friend of God and receiving attacks from satan, or maybe you think as believers in Christ, we should accept sickness because it might be sent from God to teach us something.

Let me begin with why I think Baby John's death was an attack from satan. Although the ob-gyn told me that Baby John's loss was physical and probably just chromosomes and my age, it didn't sit right in my heart. I'm not saying it wasn't physical chromosomes in the end, but what I *am* saying is I believe it was deeper than that. We know that God is the one who gives us children. It takes a man and a woman, but *God* performs the miracle of life at conception. I believe He gave us a good egg and a good sperm because He gives good gifts, and He wants us to be fruitful and multiply. Every child is a gift from God, and I could be wrong, but I believe Baby John was perfect when Jesus gave him to us. I believe something went wrong during the pregnancy. Whatever it was, I believe satan caused it because of the demonic dream I received right before I delivered his body and because I know satan doesn't want God to bless or reward us. Instead, satan is always trying to war against believers who are truly seeking after God to steal from them, kill them, and destroy them. As mature friends of God, we must look deeper at things. It's not always about the physical realm. It's not always in plain sight.

> *Every good gift and every perfect gift is from above, and comes down from the Father of lights, with whom there is no variation or shadow of turning* (James 1:17).

> *Then God blessed them, and God said to them, "Be fruitful and multiply; fill the earth and subdue it; have dominion over the fish of the sea, over the birds of the air, and over every living thing that moves on the earth"* (Genesis 1:28).

Behold, children are a heritage of the Lord, the fruit of the womb is a reward (Psalm 127:3).

The thief does not come except to steal, and to kill, and to destroy. I have come that they may have life, and that they may have it more abundantly (John 10:10).

For our struggle is not against flesh and blood [contending only with physical opponents], but against the rulers, against the powers, against the world forces of this [present] darkness, against the spiritual forces of wickedness in the heavenly (supernatural) places (Ephesians 6:12 AMP).

Now let's discuss why I do *not* think Jesus gave Julia this sickness to teach us something, but rather that it was an attack from satan. I do not believe Jesus gives people sickness and disease, at least not usually. When Jesus was on earth, He went around doing good and healing everyone who was sick and oppressed by the devil (Acts 10:38). This verse is packed full of nuggets. It not only tells us Jesus was healing people, but it also tells us who was making the people sick in the first place (oppressed by the devil). The devil was making people sick.

I do realize that people's diet and life choices can bring on sickness and death as well, accidents can happen, times of war, and so on. In addition, there is a passage in 2 Samuel, where it says the Lord struck a baby with sickness which caused him to die a week later. This was to call in the harvest of the sin David had committed with Bathsheba (2 Samuel 12:15–23). I do not have all the answers, but when Jesus was on earth, there were plenty of accounts where He did *not* cause sickness and He healed people instead. He set them free of demons and physical sickness and disease.

Later, He commissioned us believers to do the same. We see God's desire for healing to continue (Matthew 10:7–8). I'm not sure what caused the sickness that came onto Julia, but looking past the physical realm, it smelled like satan to me. I wanted Julia to be healed, and I believed Jesus did as well.

> *And as you go, preach, saying, 'The kingdom of heaven is at hand.' Heal the sick, cleanse the lepers, raise the dead, cast out demons. Freely you have received, freely give* (Matthew 10:7-8).

What Is My Weapon?

As Suzanne and I continued to walk and talk, revelation began to flow. I knew our growth in the Lord through Baby John's death was tremendous. Julia was completely fine before this. It seemed this diagnosis came on suddenly on the heels of Baby John's death. In addition, it wasn't good enough to give her one type of disease; it looked like satan had given her three types (and he made sure they were rare). For me, it became much too obvious. satan had desperately overplayed his hand.

> Side Note: I've noticed from our own lives and speaking with other friends of Jesus that if a disease comes on fast, and if it's rare, it's most likely from satan. He's trying to stop you. Don't let him.

46

Suzanne mentioned she felt this was more an attack on me, to stop me from trusting the Lord and to stop me from telling others how good God is. By faith, she said, "Julia will be fine, Katie." Based on Julia's age, Suzanne knew it was up to me to fight for Julia's healing. When I heard this, something resonated in my soul deep down. When I heard this attack was more about me than my sweet Jewels, *things just got real*.

I remember spiritually digging my heels in, squaring my shoulders, and readying myself for possibly the biggest battle I'd ever fought in my life. The feelings of helplessness fled away. Hope and determination filled my soul. I was *so* angry at satan. I'd *never* had such righteous indignation in my life! There was absolutely *no* way my daughter wasn't getting healed. She was *so* getting healed.

I looked at Suzanne like my sergeant and said, "Alright then, if this were you, if this *just* happened to your child, what would you do right now?"

She paused a minute, thinking quietly, she said, "Katie, I would go before Abba Father and ask, 'Lord, what is the strategy here, and what is my weapon against the enemy?'"

I felt such hope that night. I went home and did just that. I went before the Lord and asked those very questions. He said, "Singing praises to Me is the strategy, and your voice is the weapon. Sing Katie. Sing." Over the next few weeks and months, I sang to the Lord, and sang and sang.

The Journey Continues

Julia was now three, and we were three to four months into this diagnosis. We moved closer to UCLA and had unpacked and settled into our new home. Wanting to understand healing further, I began care-fully studying the Word of God regarding healing. In addition, I began reading books on healing by TL Osborn and Smith Wigglesworth, and I began memorizing verses on healing from the Bible.

By His stripes we are healed (Isaiah 53:5b).

For I am the Lord who heals you (Exodus 15:26b).

He sent His Word and healed them . . . (Psalm 107:20a)

My faith to receive Julia's healing grew as I read these Scriptures. Meanwhile, we were doing everything we could to hold it together. There was medication to be administered around the clock to her and much vigilance to keep her safe. Although the medication helped some-what, she was still having grand mal seizures, where she would fall to the ground or slump over, and it would begin. You had to roll her to her side, hope she didn't break any bones when falling, and make sure she wasn't swallowing her saliva or choking on it. We had to make sure she was still breathing through it. It was terrible and was still hap-pening often enough, even on medication, that Sam and I always tried to sleep with one ear open. We were exhausted.

Taylor slept in the same room as Julia and would often run into our room during the night and let us know (if we hadn't already heard). "It's happening again, Mom, Dad; come quick!" Bless Taylor's heart. She was so brave and helpful.

In addition, the medication cognitively dumbed Julia *way* down and made her very angry. It seemed our sweet peach Julia had turned into the She-Hulk overnight. She would break toys and things on purpose and rage at the drop of a hat. She would also sleep often, which was a side effect of one of the medications but also a result of having an episode. She could hardly put words together anymore. It was all present tense and very difficult to communicate with her. "I want food. Stop it. Gimme that. No. Yes."

Julia didn't seem to remember yesterday or seem to think about tomorrow. She couldn't seem to remember anyone who didn't live with us, like friends or Grandma and Grandpa. You couldn't even really talk to her about the future. "Do you want to go to the park?" She'd lose interest before you finished the sentence and would run away or break something. It was such a horrible season, physically and emotionally. We were exhausted most of the time.

Our lives had been turned upside down. We all seemed to be in survival mode, especially Sam and I. "Did you give Julia her morning meds? Where is Julia? Who left the scissors out? Put them away quick before Julia sees them. Shoot, we're an hour late for the afternoon meds. Honey, you weren't supposed to give her two pills; now it's three. Didn't I tell you? UCLA just changed it last night (again!). Do I need to get a refill today at the pharmacy, and for which med? Have you called UCLA back? She's seizing, Honey; pick her up quick! Roll her over; make sure she's breathing. Lord Jesus, help us!" Day in, day out. It felt like we were losing our sweet baby girl.

It was very challenging to know how to explain everything to Zachariah and Taylor. Their hearts were becoming numb toward their once sweet little sister. She didn't seem to care about them anymore in a loving manner or their toys and things. She would often break their things in anger and act like she didn't care. In addition, we were asking them for a lot of help and didn't have as much time to spend with them. Our hearts were breaking as we saw what was happening to our little family. We were all being stretched and pulled. Sam and I leaned heavily on Jesus for guidance and daily strength.

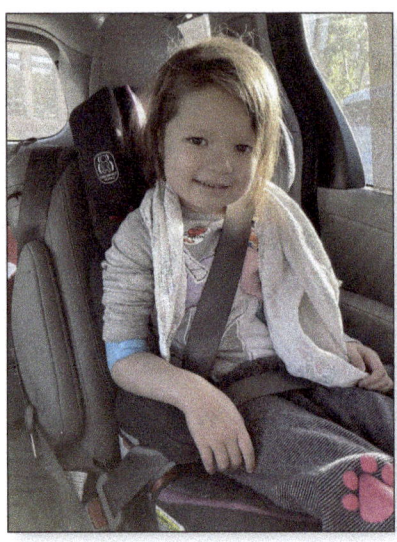

Julia after a routine blood draw. The Lord gave her such strength.

As time passed, we found a challenging but do-able routine. Meanwhile, I studied the Scriptures like crazy. I would *not* take this lying down. As the Lord instructed, I was singing to Him often, but was there anything else I could do? Some of you may be wondering . . . sing. Why sing? Well, first of all, Jesus told me to, and second, there is a story in 2 Chronicles 20, where Jehoshaphat needed God's help to beat an enemy army:

> *And when he had consulted with the people, he appointed those who should sing to the Lord, and who should praise the beauty of holiness, as they went out before the army and were saying: "Praise the Lord, For His mercy endures*

*forever." Now when they began to sing and to praise, the
Lord set ambushes against the people of Ammon, Moab,
and Mount Seir, who had come against Judah; and they
were defeated* (2 Chronicles 20:21–22).

By seeing this reflection in Scripture of what our praises could do, I knew this was God's battle, not mine. I simply had to sing. God would take care of the rest. However, being a mom who loved her daughter dearly, I wanted to make sure I covered all my bases.

> **We realized that although Julia had been diagnosed with three hard cases of epilepsy, this wasn't God's truth. It was a temporary fact that would have to change. God's truth was that Julia was healed by Jesus' stripes (Isaiah 53:5).**

In my gut, I just *knew* this was not our new normal. In the Bible, Jesus had healed people of epilepsy. He rebuked the epileptic demons out of a boy, and he was healed (Mark 9). We hadn't forgotten how Jesus healed me of a severe case of hypothyroidism. We knew He could heal Julia too. We reviewed the verses about anointing the sick with oil and praying for healing. We looked again at the verses about casting out demons. We found new verses about fasting and praying for healing. In addition to singing, we did all these things. We realized that although Julia had been diagnosed with three hard cases of epilepsy, this wasn't God's truth. It was a temporary fact that would have to change. God's truth was that Julia was healed by Jesus' stripes (Isaiah 53:5).

When folks would ask how Julia was doing, we wouldn't lie. We would let them know what the doctors were saying, but we'd remind them that according to God's Word, Julia was healed. We'd invite them to join us in praying for her healing to quickly manifest on earth as it is in heaven (Matthew 6:10).

Chapter 6

Salvation and Transformation

Interestingly enough, as we continued to administer the heavy pharmacy medication, and the anger and seizures continued, we also noticed a new heaviness coming over Julia. At this point, she had *not* accepted Jesus as her Savior yet; she was so young. All kinds of strange things began to happen. Julia would cover her ears when Sam and I would have a sermon on the TV. She never used to do that. She would say dark things like, "I don't love Jesus." She never used to say that. Something about her eyes were off and dark too. She would even look at me defiantly when I would talk about Jesus. That *never* used to happen. Finally, I realized this darkness wasn't her; it was the demons looking through her eyes right back at me, challenging me. *Why were they even there?* I thought. We kept rebuking the demons or satan as we felt led to in Jesus' name, but they kept manifesting through her actions and words. We were rebuking demons like epilepsy, anger, defiance, chaos, destruction, and so on.

> *Therefore submit to God. Resist the devil and he will flee from you* (James 4:7).

Her actions kept getting worse though. What were we doing wrong? What was I missing? The Lord showed me in Scripture:

When a demon is cast out of a person, it goes to wander in a waterless realm, searching for rest. But finding no place to rest, it says, 'I will go back and reoccupy the body I left.' When it returns, it finds the person like a house swept clean and made tidy, but empty. Then it goes and enlists seven demons more evil than itself, and they all enter and possess the person, leaving that one in a much worse state than before (Luke 11:24-26 TPT).

As a believer in Jesus Christ, when I rebuked the demons off of Julia, I believe they left. What I was missing though was that *Julia* wasn't saved. She didn't know Jesus as her personal Lord and Savior yet, and because of this, Jesus wasn't occupying her heart. I believe the demons were leaving when I rebuked them, but I also believe they came right back with more and greater demons to torment Julia because her heart was empty like the verse says – she hadn't accepted Jesus yet. The more we rebuked, the worse it got (Luke 11:24–26 above). Hence all the odd, dark, new manifestations from her.

You might wonder where all these demons were coming from. Well, in addition to epilepsy being a demon, I also believe certain heavy medications (like what we were giving Julia) can carry demons. I have no Scripture on this, just a gut feeling with firsthand experience and a word of knowledge from a friend who loves Jesus. Please be careful with certain medications, especially addictive ones. It seems they can be an open door for demons to enter a person somehow. To support this theory of pharmacy medications possibly being demonic, you can look up the word pharmacy or pharmakeia in the Strong's Dictionary:

Strong's #5331: pharmakeia (pronounced far-mak-i'-ah)
from 5332; medication ("pharmacy"), i.e. (by extension)
magic (literally or figuratively):—sorcery, witchcraft.
Thayer's Greek Lexicon:'. pharmakeia.

1) the use or the administering of drugs

2) poisoning

3) sorcery, magical arts, often found in connection
with idolatry and fostered by it

Bottom line, before you start casting out demons from someone, please learn from me, be careful to share the gospel with the person first. Explain God's love to the person and help them receive Jesus as their Savior.

Back then, I was still learning and didn't realize all this. I didn't think a three-year-old could ask Jesus into her heart. I thought she was too young, but my mom and a woman at her church both kept encouraging us to explain salvation to Julia.

In February 2020, Sam and I explained salvation to Julia. My suspicions of demonic presence were totally confirmed that day. Julia seemed to want Jesus in her heart, but there was a very evident tug-of-war going on verbally. The demons seemed to keep twisting her words and making her cry. She would begin to say Jesus, and then what she was saying would change with a different word ending. It happened again and again.

Finally, I realized what was happening—the demons didn't want to let her go. They knew if she confessed Jesus as Lord, they would have to leave and couldn't come back this time. We sang to the Lord and rebuked the demons one more time. This seemed to shut them up long enough for Julia to finally get the words out of her mouth clearly, **"Jesus is Lord!"** In that very moment, I sensed the demons flying out of her and leaving the house. She immediately began singing to Jesus, twirling around and dancing for Him. Her whole countenance changed in minutes. It was a complete supernatural transformation. Then I asked her if she believed God raised Jesus from the dead. She nodded yes.

> *That if you confess with your mouth the Lord Jesus and believe in your heart that God has raised Him from the dead, you will be saved. For with the heart one believes unto righteousness, and with the mouth confession is made unto salvation* (Romans 10:9–10).

We immediately explained water baptism to Julia, and she seemed to understand. I got her into her swimsuit and filled up the bathtub. Sam baptized her in water in front of the family as a public display of her siding with Jesus. We saw in Scripture that water baptism should follow someone's choice to follow Jesus as a public demonstration of their decision. I was not sure if this was necessary right then, but we wanted to follow God's Word the best we could.

The breakthrough was astonishing. She was kind now and gentle-spirited. She was obedient and helpful. She began singing about Jesus and enjoyed talking about Him again. Julia even began to laugh more, and began coloring shapes. Even her speech improved. The power of Jesus was truly amazing. The transformation of having Jesus in Julia's heart was supernatural.

Therefore, if anyone is in Christ, he is a new creation; old things have passed away; behold, all things have become new (2 Corinthians 5:17).

Over time, we realized the seizures continuing, but at least Julia was different. She had changed; there was no more darkness in her words or actions. We could tell that her spirit was occupied with Jesus. Thank you, Lord. As a confirmation testimony, about a week later, my friend Suzanne and I got together at a park with the kids. As Julia walked over to us to ask a question, Suzanne heard in the Spirit, "Jesus is here." Meaning as Julia approached the park bench, so did Jesus because Jesus was now living inside of Julia. Hallelujah!

We Entered His Rest

Because Julia's seizures continued, we were a little confused, but still believing for a full healing. During this season, I was listening to Kevin Zadai speak about receiving healing from Jesus.

Kevin Zadai is a strong man of God who died on the operating table and came back to life. He was with Jesus for about forty-five minutes during this time. He studies the Scripture well, and the Lord has blessed him with a huge teaching ministry. I have grown spiritually so much from listening to him teach the Word of God. He has a YouTube channel and a Warrior Notes App if you'd like to follow him.

Kevin has received several healings himself. He mentioned that sometimes, even though demons leave when rebuked, the disease they brought could have become organic. At that point, you may still need healing from the Lord. To clarify what he was saying, I saw in Scripture with the epileptic that Jesus specifically asked the father how long the boy had suffered with this disease (perhaps deciding the route He must take to deliver and heal him?). Jesus rebuked the demon, and then He reached down and helped the boy up (Mark 9). Perhaps a two-step process? I'm not sure.

My sister Sally came along side us through this entire process and diligently prayed for Julia to be healed. She had a prophetic word from the Lord that Julia would be fine, that she would not only be healed of this fowl disease but would also cognitively catch up to where you couldn't tell it ever happened. Also, that God would use her testimony to encourage others. Hallelujah! What encouragement this was to us.

In my gut, I knew the Lord would heal Julia because He said she was healed in His Word, and He does not lie. The Word of knowledge through Sally confirmed this as well. For months and months, I kept studying the Scriptures on healing, and we continued practicing what we saw in Scripture: we'd lay hands on Julia and pray for healing. We kept rebuking epilepsy in Jesus' name, fasted, prayed, and sang to Jesus. We anointed her with oil, had our pastor pray over her, and had a prophet pray over her. We sang and sang and praised the Lord.

> *And these signs will follow those who believe: In My name they will cast out demons; they will speak with new tongues; they will take up serpents; and if they drink any-thing deadly, it will by no means hurt them; they will lay hands on the sick, and they will recover* (Mark 16:17–18).

> *Is anyone among you sick? Let him call for the elders of the church, and let them pray over him, anointing him with oil in the name of the Lord. And the prayer of faith will save the sick, and the Lord will raise him up. And if*

he has committed sins, he will be forgiven. Confess your trespasses to one another, and pray for one another, that you may be healed. The effective, fervent prayer of a righteous man avails much (James 5:14–16).

And when He had come into the house, His disciples asked Him privately, "Why could we not cast it out?" So He said to them, "This kind can come out by nothing but prayer and fasting" (Mark 9:28-29).

Then about a year into all of this, the Lord showed me this verse in my quiet time with Him:

When I select an appointed time, I will judge with equity," [says the Lord] (Psalm 75:2 AMP).

It jumped right off the page into my heart. I thought, *Okay, we're getting somewhere. Praise God! You will just pick a day, and that's that. Julia will be healed. Hallelujah!* I believe it was Kevin Zadai who taught me to return God's Word to Him while waiting for a healing and thank Him for it as though it were already done. I finally relaxed a bit and stopped striving. I stopped running Julia around for more folks to lay hands on her. I put my "jug" of anointing oil away. I entered a mode of rest and confidence in my Savior and kept singing to God and thanking Him for healing Julia. I kept speaking like it had already happened out loud and believing it 100 percent.

Instead of begging and pleading with God to heal our sweet baby girl, I began confidently returning God's Word to Him daily. As I would give Julia the medication, I would say, "Thank you, Lord, for healing

Julia." "Please bring your will to earth (her healing), as it is in heaven."
I framed our future by the words of my mouth and the faith in my heart.

For as the rain comes down, and the snow from heaven, and do not return there, but water the earth, and make it bring forth and bud, that it may give seed to the sower and bread to the eater, So shall My word be that goes forth from My mouth; it shall not return to Me void, but it shall accomplish what I please, and it shall prosper in the thing for which I sent it (Isaiah 55:10–11).

Your kingdom come, your will be done, on earth as it is in heaven (Matthew 6:10).

According to your faith let it be done to you (Matthew 9:29b).

For I am the Lord who heals you (Exodus 15:26b).

He sent His word and healed them . . . (Psalm 107:20a).

I have heard your prayer, I have seen your tears; surely I will heal you (2 Kings 20:5b).

By His stripes we are healed (Isaiah 53:5b).

> **Even though life wasn't peaceful physically, our hearts found peace mentally.**

Although we were still administering medication around the clock to Julia because the healing hadn't manifested yet, the Lord had *so* transformed my husband and I to trust Him that we entered a mode of rest. Even though life wasn't peaceful physically, our hearts found peace mentally.

> *You will keep him in perfect peace, whose mind is stayed on You, because he trusts in You* (Isaiah 26:3).

> *There remains therefore a rest for the people of God. For he who has entered His rest has himself also ceased from his works as God did from His* (Hebrews 4:9–10).

At this point, Sam and I finally began talking through our loss of Baby John and whether we'd like to ever try again for another baby. It was healing on all fronts to talk through things and process them together. Because of Julia's diagnosis so close to John's move to heaven, I guess we never made time to talk about it in a healthy way. We were just in survival mode for so long. After talking things over, we both felt ready to try again and became pregnant that fall.

Chapter 7

Baby Esther and Christmas Cookies

I was over the moon to be pregnant again! I'd always wanted a big family and had cried so many times over the loss of our sweet Baby John. Although a very rocky season with Julia's diagnosis, we were waiting quietly and confidently now to receive her healing from the Lord. He set our feet on solid ground. It seemed that God was now restoring what the locusts had eaten (Joel 2:25).

I found out on July 17, 2019, that Baby John was in heaven, and when I went to my first doctor's appointment for this new pregnancy, the doctor gave me the due date of July 17, 2021. I saw the date on the monitor, and it jumped off the screen right into my soul. It was a *huge* hug from heaven. God loves numbers, and I knew He wasn't replacing Baby John, but I felt He was acknowledging our loss and redeeming the date with this new baby.

Side Note: If you see a date returning or being redeemed to you, make sure to thank Jesus. He does so many special things for us if we are paying attention.

I ordered *Big Brother* and *Big Sister* t-shirts for the kids and bought Mom and Dad some *Grandma and Grandpa Again* mugs. It was so fun! I was giddy and so full of joy.

Baby Esther on Board

One morning in the first trimester, I felt a little tight as I took my usual walk around the neighborhood but didn't think anything of it. Then later that day, I showed definite signs of miscarriage. My heart was rocked! I was in shock. I raced to the ob-gyn the next day or two and was so relieved to hear our sweet baby's heartbeat for the first time! The doctor said just walk less and take it easy. He also gave me progesterone pills in case my progesterone needed a boost. I drove home happily and raced into the house holding up the ultrasound pictures and declaring, "We're having a baby!" Sam and the kids knew I was pregnant, but when I left for the doctor's office that morning, things were still up in the air from the bleeding. We had a *huge* family hug and a joyful afternoon together.

All that week I rested, which is *very* hard to do as a homeschool momma. Sam and the kids were extremely gracious. They brought me things, and we did school on the couch the best we could. But no matter how much I rested and we prayed, the bleeding continued steadily. God had given me a sign by the baby's due date being July 17th, and I hung onto that by faith declaring life over the baby often. I kept declaring the blood of Jesus over my womb and the baby and our whole family.

Three weeks into my bed rest, about 4 or 5 a.m., I sat up in bed and was about to use the restroom when I heard a demon screaming loudly as it left the house. At the same time, a terrible amount of blood flow left me. At that point, I knew satan or his demons had been attacking my womb again. About six hours later, with tears running down my face, I miscarried the baby's body at home. Sam was at work, and the kids were playing in the other room.

There are no words for what I felt in those moments. All alone in the bathroom, I pulled the sweet baby's body out of the toilet, holding it tenderly. I couldn't stop sobbing. Then out of my gut came a song that surprised even me. Through muffled tears and cracks in my voice, I sang, "God is so good . . . God is so good . . ." I believe my spirit took over in those moments to let my mind still know that God was good, and that He loved me. He did not do this to me.

Moments later in the shower, I remember the dam of tears breaking. I just kept sobbing and banging my fists against the shower wall. "No, God! No! Not again! How did this happen again?" Later, I called my husband and told him what had happened. He came right home and gave me the biggest hug I can ever remember. We held each other for a while and cried together.

The LORD is close to the brokenhearted and saves those who are crushed in spirit (Palms 34:18 NIV).

God was so gentle with me. He gave me a verse right away:

I will establish your seed forever . . . (Psalm 89:4a AMP).

We like to name our children, even if they go right to heaven. This one being so small (about nine weeks along), it was hard to tell if the baby was a boy or girl. We asked the Lord for a sign. Through various numbers and ways, He showed me she was a girl and that her name was Esther. So that is what we named her, Esther Lopez. My spirit knows she is an amazing cook and is very brave.

I know God's intent was for Esther to live in this earth; I know it with all of my being. Her due date spoke volumes to me, but the verse John 10:10 says, "The thief does not come except to steal, and to kill, and to destroy. I have come that they may have life, and that they may have it more abundantly." I just kept telling myself, "What the enemy means for evil, my God will turn for good" (Genesis 50:20). Even with these truths, the tears kept coming. My heart was broken.

Soul Healing

I went to the doctor afterward, and he examined me. Although a different doctor this time, I heard the same thing again. "Everything looks normal; no reason for the miscarriage . . . probably chromosomes." He was very kind and encouraged Sam and I to try again if we wanted to. But he certainly didn't find any physical reason for the miscarriage.

I didn't want to fall into depression or self-pity over the loss of yet another baby. Over the past year of studying God's Word for Julia's healing, I had drawn very close to the Lord in many ways. One of the things God taught me during this time was how to heal my soul. Some of you may know exactly what I'm talking about, while others may not.

We are made in three parts, just like God is three-in-one (God, Jesus, Holy Spirit). We are spirit, soul, and body.

> *Now may the God of peace Himself sanctify you com-*
> *pletely; and may your whole spirit, soul, and body be pre-*
> *served blameless at the coming of our Lord Jesus Christ*
> (1 Thessalonians 5:23).

When we ask Jesus into our heart, our **spirit** is instantly saved, and we become a new creation in Jesus Christ. "Therefore, if anyone is in Christ, he is a new creation; old things have passed away; behold, all things have become new" (2 Corinthians 5:17). Then we live the rest of our lives sanctifying our **soul** in Christ Jesus (making our mind, will, and emotions more like Christ; Romans 8). Finally, our **body** follows our mind. If we think healthy thoughts, renew our mind on truths from God's Word, and make wise choices with food and drink, our body will prosper (3 John 2).

Instead of carrying all this pain and trauma for months in my heart (my mind) as I did after losing Baby John, I felt the Holy Spirit nudging me to heal my soul right after Baby Esther. I was so sad that I think I waited a day or two. Finally, I said, "Yes Lord, I will obey."

Here is what I did and how it works:

"Lord, I loose all pain, trauma, sorrow, sadness, disappointment, anger, and sense of loss from my soul in Jesus' name. Lord, I bind God's love, joy, and hope to my soul in Jesus' name."

Here is the verse to support this prayer:

> *I will give you the keys (authority) of the kingdom of*
> *heaven; and whatever you bind [forbid, declare to be*

improper and unlawful] on earth will have [already]
been bound in heaven, and whatever you loose [permit,
declare lawful] on earth will have [already] been loosed
in heaven (Matthew 16:19 AMP).

It was like a deep breath of fresh air flowed into my soul that day. I literally felt like I was lifted up higher. My thoughts and emotions were supernaturally healed at a great rate, seconds after saying that prayer. I felt like I was flying high like an eagle (emotionally). Joy came back to me almost instantly. Not that I wasn't sad. Of course I was still sad, but my hope and overall joy in the Lord came back to me in moments. It was supernatural.

But those who wait on the Lord shall renew their strength;
They shall mount up with wings like eagles, they shall
run and not be weary, they shall walk and not faint
(Isaiah 40:31).

Later that week, I felt so much better that I was even able to make Christmas cookies with the kids and deliver them to the neighbors. From that prayer, Jesus was able to supernaturally heal my heart from this trauma so quickly that I was able to think about others and actually got up and served them with honest joy. I don't say this pridefully; I say it to give God the glory.

Side Note: If you are struggling with pain from past trauma, loss, or grief, just say out loud a similar declaration as I did above. The Lord will work supernaturally in your heart and mind to heal you. If you are aware of any sin, confess that first. The key is to

loose whatever is wrong and bind the opposite in Jesus' name. I learned this prayer from Kat Kerr. She is an amazing woman of God. She has a YouTube channel and website if you want to learn more.

Julia and I giving Christmas cookies to the neighbors

God wants us to be emotionally and physically healed from things like this, but we must let Him help us. I still cry now and then about the babies in heaven, but it's not a deep, heavy, depths-of-despair cry. It is simply sadness about missing my babies. However, my soul was healed that day, and satan was never able to pull me into depression or anything worse. I know I will see my precious Esther and John again someday in heaven. That always puts a pep in my step.

For those of you who have lost a baby in the womb or a young child and are not sure about where their spirit went, I believe babies and children go straight to heaven when they pass away. If you are a believer in Jesus Christ, when you pass from this earth, you will see your baby again in heaven. Hallelujah! King David in the Bible talks about this. He spoke of his child who passed away shortly after birth. He prayed and fasted for him to become well, but the baby died. He speaks of seeing him again in heaven some day.

> *But now he is dead; why should I fast? Can I bring him back again? I shall go to him, but he shall not return to me* (2 Samuel 12:23).

Six Chairs and a Table

As the days went on, I began to ask the Lord hard questions like, "Did we do the right thing, God? Did you want us to have more children? The desire in our hearts for a bigger family—is that just Sam and I? Or is it coming from you, Lord? Two losses in a row now, God; are we hearing you right? Even though it feels like satan has been taking these children, are we missing something?" I didn't hear anything right away from God, so I asked for a clear sign in the natural, something I couldn't make up, something obvious to say, "Yes, Katie, I do want you to have a big family. It's not all in your head." Later that morning, the sign arrived by way of a furniture delivery truck.

Back when we were still pregnant with Esther, we ordered a new table. In all our years of marriage, we'd never had a brand new table.

With Esther on the way (back then), I figured it was time for a nice, big table with six chairs. After all, we were going to be a family of six, right? The delivery was quite a bit later than when we ordered it due to covid. So mid-December, *after* Esther moved to heaven, the table arrived. Bittersweet. Yes. And to rub it in like salt to a wound, the head delivery man came to me and said, "Oh Miss, we have your table, but for some reason, we only have five chairs today. I'm sorry." In my head, I was like, *You've got to be kidding me. What, did the table miscarry too?* I mean, in my heart, that sixth chair represented the sixth person in our family (on earth). The delivery man's comment really stung. He, of course, had no idea what was going on in my head.

Finally, my practical side kicked in, knowing we'd paid for six chairs, I questioned him firmly, "But the sixth chair *will be* delivered at some point, correct?"

He quickly agreed. "Oh yes, Ma'am; it's just back-ordered."

My heart just about skipped a beat! I instantly knew that was my answer from Jesus, and the sign in the natural that I couldn't deny. Yes, we *did* hear God correctly. He did want us to have more children, and I'm sure He wanted us to have John and Esther too, but at this point, just like our dining room chair, the next child was on back order.

Chapter 8

The Whirlwind and Miraculous Healing

It was January of 2021 now, and Julia was about four-years-old. One day as I journaled with the Lord, He told me He had a "suddenly" coming for Sam and I. Thanking Him, I went about my day. Spring comes early in Southern California, so by February, I was already able to garden.

On February 27, 2021, I was working in the backyard with the garden. Suddenly, over my head in the sky, but close it seemed, I heard a *huge* sound like the wind going eighty miles an hour! I quickly ducked, thinking something was about to hit my head. I looked up and saw nothing. Nothing was even blowing in the breeze or moving above me. *Very strange,* I thought. Then it stopped. Puzzled, I began to walk across the yard a few paces. There it was again! Another *huge* sound like a mighty rushing wind or a 747 right above me. I could hear it whirling around, right above me! I looked up again, still nothing. It stopped again. In my gut I knew it had to do with Julia's healing, but I couldn't put my finger on how. I thought I was hearing in the natural, but later the Lord revealed that no—I was hearing in the spirit; it was coming from the other realm. I started delving into Scripture after Scripture on whirlwind sounds and what they meant.

Why did I look into Scripture to find the answer? I had just been listening to a teaching by Robin Bullock, and he said something about the amount of your revelation from God depends on how much of the Bible you understand. I believe he was saying that God has given us *much* more information in the Bible than we realize. The more we read and understand it, the more the Lord can reveal to us not only His truths but also His mysteries. There is much hidden in the Word of God, but He is not in the business of handing out pearls to swine (Matthew 7:6). We must be hungry, digging to find these precious truths in God's Word. You can find more information about Robin Bullock on his YouTube channel and website.

In addition to studying the Bible, I have found that the closer my friendship is with the Lord, the more revelation He will give me. Mr. Zadai mentions this. I believe certain revelation or understanding is based on our intimacy (closeness) with the Lord. It makes sense. Do you tell your secrets to just anyone? Of course not. You only tell secrets to the friends you trust. The same is true with the Lord.

> *Do not give what is holy to the dogs; nor cast your pearls before swine, lest they trample them under their feet, and turn and tear you in pieces* (Matthew 7:6).

> *He rewards those who earnestly seek Him* (Hebrews 11:6b).

> *He made known His ways to Moses, His acts to the children of Israel* (Psalm 103:7).

> *So the Lord spoke to Moses face to face, as a man speaks to his friend* (Exodus 33:11a).

Why do you think Jesus spoke in so many parables while on earth? Then He would end with, "He that has ears to hear, let him hear." Matthew 13 explains in more detail, but I believe Jesus wanted to make sure the mysteries and gems He was teaching were appreciated and taken in by those who were truly hungry and seeking Him. I knew that by digging into the Word of God, I would find what I was looking for, the mystery or treasure of the whirlwind.

Sure enough, Mr. Bullock was right! After a week or so of asking Holy Spirit and searching the Scriptures, the Lord showed me a couple of passages on the whirlwind: one on the day of Pentecost and another with Job (Acts 2 and Job 38). In Acts 2, the Holy Spirit comes suddenly in a mighty rushing wind (which is what I believe I heard), and in Job 38, the Lord speaks from a whirlwind. I did not hear an audible voice speaking, but in both passages, it's clear that the Holy Spirit or the Lord can come in a rushing wind or a whirlwind. It certainly appeared then that the Lord came to our house that day in the whirlwind, but did He heal Julia when He came?

In answer to this question, the Lord gently walked me back through my journal notes to confirm that yes, He indeed healed Julia when He came in the whirlwind that day. He reminded me that He would select an appointed time and judge with equity (Psalm 75:2). He then showed me that February 27, 2021, *was* the appointed time. He showed me it was His Jewish holiday called Purim, which means Divine Reversal (book of Esther). Hallelujah! God couldn't have been more clear! And what a beautiful festival to heal Julia on: the Divine Reversal. What the enemy meant for evil, God turned around for good (Genesis 50:20).

Pharmakeia

Now that we believed Julia was healed, we faced the same decision I did when my thyroid was healed. What do we do with the heavy medication? I remembered the Lord asking me to go off my medication immediately when He healed my thyroid, but this was somehow different. The medication we were giving Julia was stronger, and there was more of it. All the articles I read about going off the medication she was on said to wean slowly. At the time, I believe she was on three different epilepsy management medications per UCLA's instruction, and we were giving them to her multiple times a day. We sought the Lord in prayer. This was serious; it wasn't our body but our precious four-year-old's. Sam and I agreed that she was healed, but the only way to prove it would be to see her off meds and doing fine with no seizures and full cognitive restoration (speaking, drawing, walking, and running properly—the disease had affected so much).

Around that time, my mom's friend from church had a vision of a snake wrapped around Julia's head with the word *Pharmakeia*. This friend said, "Take Julia off the meds; she'll be fine." This man loves Jesus very much. Although not a doctor, I trusted his vision as being from the Lord to guide us in answer to our prayers for wisdom. In addition, Julia's side effects from a prior new medication were terrible. She was doing so poorly that Sam and I had already been discussing lowering at least one of them with or without UCLA's approval.

We'd been around the block with various kinds of medication for Julia: up, down, new ones, old ones. Some seemed to control the seizures better than others. Others seemed to affect her cognitively or emotionally worse than others. UCLA kept trying to find the "sweetspot." We normally always followed their advice, but at this point, especially believing Julia to be healed, we began to lower her medication. We started later that day of the whirlwind. Then in the days to follow, Holy Spirit pressed me to continue to remove more and more medication. This was without UCLA's approval or knowledge. Not that doctors and medicine are all bad; God uses them at times to heal, but from working with UCLA for a while, we knew they would not agree with or believe a miracle had happened. Even if we could convince them, we knew they certainly wouldn't approve lowering *all* the medication this quickly. However, I could hear the Holy Spirit very clearly, and I knew He was asking us to lower all medication and double time!

> *But Peter and the other apostles answered and said: "We ought to obey God rather than men"* (Acts 5:29).

In addition, God kept reminding me of Mom's friend's vision of the snake and the medication being the problem now, not the disease. This was an incredible leap of faith for Sam and I, but we obeyed God and quickly lowered all the medication.

During the forty to fifty days it took to wean Julia off all medication, it became very evident that she was truly healed. She kept acting and sounding better every time we'd lower more. The entire time, there were *no* seizures. None. This was not normal because in the past, whenever we'd adjust medications up or down by UCLA's direction, there were several seizures or new symptoms as her system would adjust. At this point, we knew for sure God had miraculously healed our baby girl!

We will thank Him forever for restoring our precious Julia Rose to us. He even put the icing on the healing cake: the very first day Julia was medication free was on Resurrection Sunday! What symbolism.

We felt Jesus brought her back to life emotionally. She was our sweet baby girl again; such a comedian, such a joy, and so kind and smart. The real Julia was back!

Julia could talk normally again and was so full of joy and smiles. You could talk with her about the future or the past. She could finally understand and keep up! She even remembered Grandma and Grandpa and was so kind to Zach and Taylor. She wasn't angry anymore either, and her cognitive abilities just kept advancing and catching up to her natural age.

Zachariah and Taylor drew closer to Julia as well; they learned to trust and respect her again. They loved her on a whole new level. You could see and hear it in their speech and play. They included her in their games and playtime. The Lord was redeeming us on all fronts. He was bringing our family back together physically, mentally, and emotionally!

First few days after Resurrection Sunday. Julia fully healed and off meds!

About a month later—you can see the joy back in her eyes!

Chapter 9

Bonfire and a Good Show

We were privileged to have my mom staying with us during this time. She too, had been praying and believing God to heal Julia. She was so excited about the miraculous healing. Shortly afterward, I said, "Mom, I want to burn the rest of the medication. Let's have a victory bonfire."

She immediately agreed, "Let's do it!"

Sam and I got a bonfire going in our backyard, and we poured bottle after bottle of the remaining pharmacy pills into the flames. I wanted *nothing* left of it. We roasted what satan meant for evil to ashes. God is so very, very good.

> *The thief does not come except to steal, and to kill, and to destroy. I have come that they may have life, and that they may have it more abundantly* (John 10:10).

Grandma Cindi (my mom) and Julia

We enjoyed "crunching" satan under our feet that night as the medication melted into the flames. In my mind, the medication represented the snake-demon in Mom's friend's vision. I couldn't resist. I had to get rid of it all in a complete way.

> *Behold, I give you the authority to trample on serpents*
> *and scorpions, and over all the power of the enemy, and*
> *nothing shall by any means hurt you* (Luke 10:19).

About a week later, the Lord thinned the veil between the physical and supernatural realms and gave us a really good show. At the time, we lived in the rolling hills north of Los Angeles. Very hot, dry, and lots of brush; it was easy for critters to hang out in the brush. We had a fenced-in backyard, and for the most part, the critters (coyotes, snakes, and squirrels) stayed where they were, and we stayed where we were. However, that day Julia was in the backyard playing happily on the trampoline when she saw a snake inside the fence. She pointed it out to my mom. I heard Mom scream as she grabbed Julia off the trampoline. All of us gathered inside the house and watched from the sliding glass window as the snake was trying to fight with a squirrel; both were bleeding and moving slowly. So strange. We figured they must've been fighting up on the nearby hill and brought the tussle down into our backyard without realizing it.

The squirrel lunged for the snake; the snake tried to lunge back. Both were still bleeding and moving slowly. Not sure what to do, I called our pest control. "Nope—sorry Ma'am, we don't have the right equipment today to come kill a snake for you." Then I called Sam at work, no answer. He was on position and had to turn his phone off. *Okay great,* I thought. *We have a bleeding snake fighting a crazy squirrel in our backyard. What is going on?* This had never happened before, and we'd lived there a while. I was still thinking only in the natural.

At some point, the squirrel took off, so our focus was only on the snake. We called our neighbor who knew all about snakes. I sent her some pictures, and she helped us decide it was *not* a rattle snake. He was not rattling and did not have the right patterns on his back. Okay, that was helpful, but still . . . what were we going to do with it? The kids, Mom, and I gathered around the dining room table, trying to decide. The snake was still not leaving. Zachariah begged me to let him try and kill it. "No, son. It's too dangerous." I said as I half-listened, mostly thinking, *Where is my dear husband when I need him? Working . . . Oh yes, that's right. Good man.*

Peeking out the window again, we realized the snake had made his way over to the back patio couch. He crawled up into it and began resting in the sunshine. Not cool. That's when I started to boil a little. How *dare* that filthy thing get comfy *right* where I drink my coffee and relax outside? This was *not* okay with me.

Meanwhile, my ten-year-old son, Zachariah, was still begging me to give him a shot at killing the snake. Until now, I hadn't really been listening. Suddenly, my spiritual ears were opened. Zach said, "Momma, you *know* I've been practicing with lizards this past year. I've killed so many! I'm a good shot, Momma. I'm sure I could get this snake too." In all fairness, my son was right. We saw hundreds of small lizards on our property annually. They would scurry here and there all the time. For fun, my son had been popping them with his heavy-duty nerf gun and feeding them to the chickens; good protein for them, you know. He had become a pretty good aim.

As my spiritual ears began to open, the Holy Spirit translated what Zach's heart was saying: "King Saul, you *know* I've killed a lion and a bear. I just *know* I can kill this giant too." It was the story of when young David killed Goliath, a giant (1 Samuel 17:36). *Ding.* God finally got through to me.

Trusting the Lord, I sighed, "Son, have at him. Be safe." I did not ask for details on how he would go about it. I just trusted the Lord. After a rousing couple of rounds, Zach killed the snake! Hallelujah!

Zachariah killed the snake! Thank you, Jesus!

I realized later that God was letting us see in the natural whatever snake was in my mom's friend's vision. It was now dead in the supernatural *and* dead in the natural. *We had total victory!* Hallelujah! It was an intense but good show from the Lord.

To this day, we are thanking God for healing our precious daughter, Julia Rose. After being healed, for the next month or two, she rapidly increased in sentence structure. She was thinking more clearly and finding her words easily. She began running and walking normally, and even began to color and sit longer for story time. Just like the Lord spoke through my sister Sally, you can't even tell that anything happened. She's completely normal and set free!

Chapter 10

Double for Our Trouble

One thing I haven't touched on yet regarding my desire for a big family is that I've always wanted twins. For years, I have been praying for twins, even declaring for them out loud by faith.

> *You will also declare a thing, and it will be established for you; So light will shine on your ways* (Job 22:28).

> *A man will be satisfied with good by the fruit of his mouth*
> . . . (Proverbs 12:14a).

Side Note: If you're not sure about declarations, please look at Psalm 72, where King David declares and prays beautiful things over his son, King Solomon. Many, if not all, come to pass for King Solomon. Our words really do matter. On the flip side, we will also be held accountable for every idle or careless word we say (Matthew 12:36). God listens to our words. He created the universe by speaking. We are made in God's image, so He has made our words powerful as well.

I believe the Lord gave me this strong desire for twins, specifically, a boy and a girl. I felt it was just a matter of time until the Lord would bless us with them. For years, each time I became pregnant, I'd get excited for the first baby appointment; I would hope this would be the pregnancy where the ultrasound nurse would say, "Oh my—I see two heartbeats!" After what happened with John and Esther, I began declaring double-for-my-trouble verses.

> *Instead of your shame you shall have double honor, and instead of confusion they shall rejoice in their portion. Therefore in their land they shall possess double; everlasting joy shall be theirs* (Isaiah 61:7).

> *Return to the stronghold, you prisoners of hope. Even today I declare that I will restore double to you* (Zechariah 9:12).

Now that Julia was healed, it felt like God was quickly moving down His list of recompense for our family. Signs for twins seemed to pop up everywhere: billboards, a truck with twins on the advertising, and Sam had a dream from the Lord about twins. Then the Lord dropped a song into my heart from *For King & Country*, "Priceless," but only certain words from the song kept playing over and over in my head for a day or two.

> *"Sisters, we can start again*
> *Give honor 'til the end*
> *Love, we can start again*
> *Brothers, we can start again*
> *Give honor 'til the end*

Yeah, we can start again."

I like the song, but these lines normally didn't stand out to me more than any other part of the song. Why were *these* lines replaying over and over in my head? I asked the Lord what they meant.

Side Note: I've learned the Lord or angels will sing over you when they are trying to get your attention or direct your thoughts, especially if it's repeated. So please listen if you are hearing something in your spirit on "replay." If you're not sure, ask Holy Spirit what the song, verse, or phrase means. He will let you know. The Lord is trying to communicate with us all the time.

The Lord your God in your midst, the Mighty One, will save; He will rejoice over you with gladness, He will quiet you with His love, He will rejoice over you with singing (Zephaniah 3:17).

Let's look at the lyrics again, see if you can pick up what the Lord was trying to tell me:

"Sisters, we can start again
Give honor 'til the end
Love, we can start again
Brothers, we can start again
Give honor 'til the end
Yeah, we can start again."

The Lord didn't reply directly. I sensed He was just smiling at me, waiting for me to get it. Earlier that week, I thought maybe I felt some pregnancy symptoms but was trying not to get excited. Then the song lyrics and pregnancy symptoms collided in my mind! Yes! He was trying to tell me we were gonna "start again," as some folks say, with a baby. But it wasn't just a baby; it was a sister and a brother. *"Sisters, we can start again . . . Brothers, we can start again . . ."* I finally got it. What a fun way to tell me, Jesus! Thank you.

My heart soared. Shortly afterward, I took a pregnancy test, and it was positive. Sometimes in early pregnancy, I have felt the implantation of the baby. With this pregnancy, I felt two different implantations, about twelve hours apart. I was ridiculously excited. A couple of weeks later, I was already showing. Everything seemed to be happening so fast.

During that time, I went to our ladies' Bible study from church; as prayer requests were taken, I asked for prayer for a healthy pregnancy. Everyone was so excited for me. One of the ladies had a word of knowledge from the Lord for me. Although I didn't know her well, she said after we prayed, "I'm hearing twins . . . in fact, I believe I heard a boy and a girl?" She asked if that made sense or resonated with me.

Astounded, I quickly said, "Yes! I've been praying for a boy and girl twin for years." She loves the Lord very much and had no idea about my desire for twins. That word from the Lord was so confirming and encouraging to me. I'm so grateful she yielded to the Holy Spirit and spoke up.

Side Note: Words of knowledge and other gifts of the Spirit can be found in 1 Corinthians 12. They're meant for the edification of the body of Christ and also to win the lost, as Jesus did with the woman at the well in John 4.

I quickly brought down my pregnancy clothes from the closet, and we started planning for two precious additions to our family.

Flying in the Spirit

About six weeks into the pregnancy, the Lord woke me around 4 a.m. with these words, "Fast and pray for twenty-one days." There was urgency in His voice. I got right up and sat before the Lord. He explained it was a Daniel fast—to fast something every day for twenty-one days. He said it was for the babies and to pray the evil one's plans would be thwarted. I knew there must be an attack happening in the supernatural against my womb again, so I prayed earnestly.

About 5 or 6 a.m., I became very sleepy. He told me to lie down and sleep. As I slumped over onto a pillow on the couch, I entered a dream state and began to feel the Lord's presence all around me. Warmth enveloped me, and there were waves of love flowing over me again and again. I was held securely by angels, or Jesus, I wasn't sure.

Then in the body or in the spirit, I don't know, we began to lift off the couch. I can't explain it exactly, but I was lifted out of the house. My spirit knew we were passing through the roof and then up over the house. We continued for a bit. Then the snug, warm waves of love started to fade gently, and I found myself back on the couch. I woke up smiling and laughing quietly. I will explain what I think happened in a bit.

> *And I know such a man—whether in the body or out of the body I do not know, God knows* (2 Corinthians 12:3).

Later that morning as we were preparing for church, I used the restroom and found signs of miscarriage. My heart sank and I remember saying, "No!" A very helpless feeling washed over me as I began to cry. I thought I had been resting during this pregnancy. I thought I'd been so careful; taking my vitamins and not overdoing it. I told Sam, and he and the kids all gathered around me. We prayed and sang together, asking the Lord to spare the twins.

We decided to still go to church. I wasn't going to let fear stop me from serving. I was to play piano that morning on the worship team as well as teach in Sunday school. Tears kept welling up as I worshiped the Lord that morning on the piano. Blinking them back, I kept praying in my heart.

After church, I remember slowly pushing chairs back into the table as I cleaned up the Sunday school room, knowing I needed to sit down. Knowing what was most likely happening physically, I couldn't keep the dam of tears back any longer. My husband told a few people at church, and they came to pray with us for healing and for life in my womb. As we pulled into the driveway at home, my pants were soaked through. I changed quickly and rested, but in my heart, I knew it must be over. I rested all the next day as well. At one point, Zachariah and I were praying together, and he said, "Momma, I see two heartbeats in your tummy." I agreed, "Yes, sweetheart. I know the babies want to live. Let's keep praying."

I scheduled an appointment with the doctor the next morning, but he couldn't see me for another three to four days. During the wait, Sam had a dream. It was from the Lord, but it was a tough one. Without going into detail, a demon-reaper-like creature was taking the life of our male goat. At the time, we had goats. We had one male and two female goats. Our goal was to breed them, sell the baby goats when they were weaned, and then have milk, cheese, yogurt, and so on.

At this point, our male goat was about three to four months old. He hadn't become a daddy yet because he was still growing up. In the dream, Sam said he felt helpless because he was unable to get to Eddie in time (our male goat). He said in the dream, "There go our future generations." I knew exactly what this statement meant; satan or a demon was after our children in the womb again! He was stealing our future generations.

> *For our struggle is not against flesh and blood [contending only with physical opponents], but against the rulers, against the powers, against the world forces of this [present] darkness, against the spiritual forces of wickedness in the heavenly (supernatural) places* (Ephesians 6:12 AMP).

Side Note: When asking God to help you interpret your dreams, pay special attention to what people said or what you said in the dream. Usually, what is said is key to the meaning of the dream.

A couple days later, I earnestly watched the monitor as the doctor looked around for any life in my womb. He shook his head sadly, "I'm so sorry . . . nothing here. You must have had a miscarriage again." He looked for any physical signs that may have caused the miscarriage. "Everything looks good. No problems at all." Smiling kindly, he looked at Sam, "We know you must be fine. She keeps getting pregnant." Sam chuckled, and I tried to smile. The doctor gave us some mild encouragement to keep trying if we wanted more children. Although three miscarriages in a row now, he mentioned it doesn't mean the end.

The doctor went on about my age (forty-one) and how 50 percent of my eggs must be bad. I'd heard it all before. I politely half-smiled, but in my heart, I didn't agree. I kept thinking about the dream God gave Sam with the demon and the goat; I also understand many women in their forties can have healthy children. No disrespect to doctors or to this particular doctor. He is very kind, but I believe the Lord gives good eggs and sperm (James 1:17). Something could have gone wrong physically in the end, but I believe satan caused it.

In my gut, I sensed satan hated that Julia was healed. He's not stupid, he saw the whirlwind. He knew we'd become closer friends of God, and that we were telling others how much God loved them. We'd been telling others to believe for their own healings as well. He hated all this I'm sure. The miscarriage felt like another attack from satan.

Although the babies were so small, and we never got to hold them physically, we still wanted to give them names. We knew their gender, so we decided to name them Joshua and Gracie. Because I didn't carry them very long, it was hard for me to get a hint of their personalities, but I know they are best friends, and I have a feeling Joshua is older, born right before Gracie.

As I quietly reflected on my flight off the couch the week before, the Lord gave me insight to why it happened. It was an answer to a question I held in my heart, but probably never verbalized to the Lord. In the past, my heart ached, wondering if Baby John or Baby Esther felt pain as they passed from this life into heaven. Now I was wondering, *Did Baby Joshua and Baby Gracie feel pain too?* I so desperately hoped there was no pain involved for them. I believe the Lord showed me what they felt for a few moments. There was no pain as I floated up. None. I felt a gentle, warm sensation of being held securely with waves of love washing over me. I thanked the Lord for this experience and answer. It brings me much comfort. If you have lost a loved one, I hope it comforts you as well. I don't believe they feel any pain as they pass from this world into the next.

> *O death, where is your victory? O death, where is your sting?* (1 Corinthians 15:55 AMP)

Chapter 11

Hard Questions and Clear Answers

Over the next few days, I realized I had become numb to life. I was so taken back and so surprised by the loss of the twins. It devastated me. I thought we were finally through all the pain, especially after the huge victory with Julia's healing! I thought we were out of the valley now. My heart really thought God was reimbursing us two-fold. What happened? If satan struck my womb again, which it certainly seemed like he did from the dream Sam had, how was he allowed to? I felt like there was some invisible test in the supernatural that I kept failing.

The closer we drew to the Lord, the harder the hits from the enemy seemed to be. At the same time, the stronger the miracle healings and supernatural encounters from the Lord became as well.

At this point, since I'd longed for the twins for so long, and now that they were in heaven, well, I entered a state of mental slow motion. I couldn't really feel anything anymore. Not really. No pain, no joy, no hope. I couldn't even cry. I went through the motions of being a mom and wife, but such pain had entered my soul. I realized that I was removing my trust in my best friend, my Savior and Lord. I began questioning why God had not intervened. I kept wondering why He allowed a third miscarriage—and twins, the ones I had prayed for, for years!

Anger welled up inside me, and the torrent of questions (and complaints) began. Haven't we suffered enough, God? The depression in Washington, Julia's diagnosis, all these miscarriages? Haven't we obeyed and trusted you through it all? Didn't you ask us to have more children, God? To what end? Shouldn't my body just hold these sweet babies full term? The doctors can't find anything wrong with me, God. What is wrong with me? Where are you? Help!

Then I clammed up. I didn't really talk to anyone for a while, thinking it would be better to process alone. Without going to the hospital, miscarrying at home can be very intense and physically overwhelming. Because of this, I believe trauma had entered my soul over the years as well as sadness. Most women I knew at the time, had no trouble in baring children, or had only one or two miscarriages at the most. Although I was not alone, I began to feel isolated in the pain and trauma I had experienced in miscarriage again and again.

At first, instead of going to Jesus for help, I tried finding articles online of ladies who had multiple miscarriages – perhaps I could relate to someone's story. Maybe I could find a believer in Christ talking about it, giving me hope, some answers. There were articles by believers in Jesus and others by those who did not believe. Most women, however, were just as confused as I was; some even blamed themselves.

Not only did the confusion come from online, but over the years, I have also heard some confusing things said to me in person or to other women going through the loss of a baby:

- *God's ways are higher than our ways.* (Essentially, don't try to figure it out).

- *Maybe something was just wrong with the baby, and God was sparing you.*

- *The Lord gives and the Lord takes a way.*

Regarding *"God's ways are higher than our ways"* (Isaiah 55:9), I think this verse may be taken out of context. This passage comes right on the heels of the Lord telling someone who has sinned to repent and that God will forgive him. I don't believe it is saying God's ways are so high that we will never understand Him. I don't believe we will ever understand all of God, but He does want us to seek Him and have an intimate relationship with Him. He desires to be our friend.

We see this with Adam and Eve in the Book of Genesis, where God actually comes down from heaven and walks and talks with them as friends. We should be able to understand *some* things about God and His ways. I believe God wants to be known by all of us, but it's those who draw close to Him, those who He calls friends, who really get to know Him.

> *For who has known the mind of the Lord that he may instruct Him? But we have the mind of Christ* (1 Corinthians 2:16).

> *He made known His ways to Moses, His acts to the children of Israel* (Psalm 103:7).

> *Draw near to God and He will draw near to you. Cleanse your hands, you sinners; and purify your hearts, you double-minded* (James 4:8).

In addition, God is not a God of confusion. He doesn't want us to be confused about Him, satan, or how things in the supernatural operate. As a believer and friend of God, I do my best to understand Him and what is happening in my life to make sure I'm following the plans He has prepared for me beforehand. I don't want to flounder and waste time. I want to know God's ways as much as possible.

> *For we are His workmanship, created in Christ Jesus for good works, which God prepared beforehand that we should walk in them* (Ephesians 2:10).

By partnering with God in this way, I have found it helps me do more for His kingdom. To partner with God, we have to hear Him clearly and obey. For me, if something doesn't reconcile (like when Julia was diagnosed with epilepsy, or after a miscarriage), I talk with God about it and see if there is something I can do to help. I do not assume I cannot understand His ways or what just happened. I may not understand completely, but I *do* ask God for wisdom and guidance.

> *If any of you lacks wisdom, let him ask of God, who gives to all liberally and without reproach, and it will be given to him* (James 1:5).

The closer I walk with the Lord, I have found the more He tells me, or perhaps the more I understand of *what* He tells me. You can see this in Scripture with Moses. He knew God's ways, but the children of Israel only knew God's acts (Psalms 103:7). Moses wanted to know God intimately, so he spent time with God, and God called Moses His friend. The children of Israel did *not* want to know God intimately, so they were *not* called God's friends, and they only knew God's acts.

As for "*God sparing me from something*" with a miscarriage, this doesn't seem quite right to me either. When a woman becomes pregnant, even from a bad situation (rape), the baby is still a life sent from God to earth, a gift. It just doesn't seem that God would take the baby (the gift) He just gave to someone right back to spare them. I will never put God in a box, and perhaps there are times when He needs to take the babies back for whatever reason. In general though, He is clear in Scripture that He wants us to be fruitful and multiply. He wants us to populate the earth.

> *So God created man in His own image; in the image of God He created him; male and female He created them. Then God blessed them, and God said to them, "Be fruitful and multiply; fill the earth and subdue it; have dominion over the fish of the sea, over the birds of the air, and over every living thing that moves on the earth"* (Genesis 1:27-28).

> *Behold, children are a heritage of the Lord, the fruit of the womb is a reward* (Psalm 127:3).

As for "*The Lord gives and the Lord takes away.*" This statement is taken from the Book of Job.

> *Then Job arose, tore his robe, and shaved his head; and he fell to the ground and worshiped. And he said: "Naked I came from my mother's womb, and naked shall I return*

there. The Lord gave, and the Lord has taken away;
Blessed be the name of the Lord (Job 1:20–21).

I've heard this verse quoted by believers in Jesus who are confused or hurt by life, and cannot quickly reconcile what is going on. I believe Job was confused and devastated, but loved God immensely. He was simply trying to submit to God which is good, but if you read further in the Book of Job, it literally tells us that satan was doing all these horrible things to Job (not God). satan was stealing from Job, killing his livestock, killing his children, and giving him physical boils. satan used various things and people to get to Job's family like robbers, lightening, a tornado, and sickness – but satan was behind it all, not God. A more accurate statement may be: *The Lord gives, and satan takes away.* Essentially, that is what John 10:10 says. Again, not that I will ever put God in a box. He may have to take babies back to heaven for certain reasons, but by and large, God wants to send babies to earth, not take them back.

> *Side note: Knowing satan's mode of operation (theft, lightening, tornados, sickness and so on) is a huge clue showing us how satan can work in our lives today. Mr. Zadai mentioned that insurance companies call some of these things (tornados, storms, hurricanes, wild fires) "Acts of God." He was explaining that this statement couldn't be farther from the truth. A more accurate statement for insurance companies to use would be, "Acts of satan."*

All that to say, reading online was confusing me, and at times well-meaning people were confusing me also with their statements of comfort. Doctors didn't seem to have the answers either. I began to review the cycle in my mind: We kept feeling nudged by God to have a bigger family. God's answer was clearly yes as He kept sending babies to us. Then it seemed satan kept taking them from us. Why? How was he allowed to? We were believers in Christ, serving God, we did our best to obey Him I thought, I kept sin out of my life, repenting of any sin I knew of. What was I missing?

Why was I so sure satan was behind the miscarriages you may ask, especially since the doctors kept telling us it was chromosomes and my age. Well, at this point I was looking deeper than just the physical realm. John 10:10 was on my mind (how God gives life, and satan often takes it), but also for us personally, during each miscarriage there was a demonic manifestation, or God would give us a dream. There was a demonic dream (with John), a loud demonic scream (with Esther), and Sam's demonic-reaper dream (with Joshua and Gracie), followed by the doctor *always* saying that everything looked good physically, no reason for the miscarriage. If not physical, then was it a spiritual problem? Was there something Sam and I could do to partner with God to stop satan from taking more babies from us?

Yes, there was, and the Holy Spirit was patiently waiting for me to turn to Him. I finally did. Then I heard His still, small voice saying, "I want to heal you, Katie, and help you . . . if you will let Me."

Soul Healing and Answers

Right after this miscarriage, I reached out to Pastor Karen, and she told me not to let depression and trauma bind me. She told me to declare, "I receive divine healing from you, Lord." When God told me He wanted to heal me, and I remembered Pastor Karen's words, I just stated it like a fact that I half-believed. I was still so hurt and confused, but I knew I was dabbling in depression and needed to start talking with the Lord again. I began our conversation with confessing depression. A freshness from Holy Spirit swept over me as God began healing my soul. From there, I slowly began to speak with Him more. I began to sing to Him too, and just breathe. I didn't address my lack of trust with Him yet; I simply began asking for wisdom and revelation. I kept going with the twenty-one-day fast.

Later, I began to address my lack of trust with Him. He took it just fine. I told God something like, "You know what, Lord? Many women have no idea why they are losing their sweet babies to miscarriage, and neither do I. Lord, please make it clear to me. I feel like I can't trust you, but I want to. I know you're not doing this to me. I believe satan is. If you will be clear with me on why we have lost so many babies in the womb, I will testify and bear witness to others. Hopefully from my testimony, we can learn the truth of what is going on."

I was expecting it to be a simple answer; it wasn't exactly simple, but He did walk me through why Sam and I had been losing babies. To be clear, I do not believe it is the same reason for everyone, but I pray by sharing our story, if perhaps you have miscarried for the same reason, that it helps you and you can learn and grow from our testimony.

> *Then Jesus said to those Jews who believed Him, "If you abide in My word, you are My disciples indeed. And you shall know the truth, and the truth shall make you free"*
> (John 8:31–32).

At the end of the twenty-one-day fast, it was Sam and my twelfth wedding anniversary. God loves dates, and for the next five to six days, God gave me dream after dream, almost nightly. It was like a *huge* anniversary gift because the dreams were mainly insight on how to help Sam and I and our family. They were packed with revelation and guidance. I understood some of the interpretations, but I went to visit Pastor Karen and her daughter Suzanne for further understanding. During this time, a friend from Mom's church also had a word of knowledge for us from the Lord. God wanted to answer my questions and to give Sam and I victory. He was using my dreams, a word of knowledge, and wisdom from friends to help us. As we put all these pieces together, the Lord was showing us that we had left a door of unconfessed sin open in our lives.

Side Note: Unconfessed sin is sin that you are aware of but have not repented of. This leaves a door open that satan can use to hurt you and your family members.

> *Do not be deceived, God is not mocked; for whatever a man sows, that he will also reap. For he who sows to his flesh will of the flesh reap corruption, but he who sows to the Spirit will of the Spirit reap everlasting life* (Galatians 6:7–8).

Sam and I were aware of the sin but didn't realize it was affecting us directly in this way. It was unconfessed anger that had grown over the years within Sam. I've spoken with Sam, and he is happy to share our story. He hopes it will help you as well.

After the military, when Sam was about twenty-five, he gave his life to Christ. Essentially, he had a lot of hurt and anger to work through from his childhood, as well as from the Marine Corps. I saw this anger working within him when we were first married and did my best to pray for him and guide him away from it. It seemed to come and go. Although he loved God very much, the anger seemed to worsen over the years. It was often fits of rage, much worse than just anger.

Things started to finally come together in my mind. Reflecting on our lives, I realized that over the years, as we grew in the Lord, satan saw our family as a threat. Looking for ways to slow us down, he began prowling for us. With unconfessed sin in our lives, we were an easy target.

> *Be sober [well balanced and self-disciplined], be alert and cautious at all times. That enemy of yours, the devil, prowls around like a roaring lion [fiercely hungry], seeking someone to devour* (1 Peter 5:8 AMP).

Because of this unconfessed anger, we were devour-able. Without repentance in this area, we left ourselves wide open to satan's attacks. As humans made in God's image (Genesis 1:27), God gave us free will. If we chose to side with anger vs. repentance, we were willfully going outside God's will and protection. Sin has consequences, and it often affects not only ourselves, but those around us.

Because of this unconfessed sin for so many years, not only did satan seem to be freely attacking my womb with miscarriage, but looking back, I realized the children were also being affected. Even though I prayed for protection from the Lord, and had no unconfessed sin in my own life, things kept happening to us. Zachariah, Julia, and I started to have intense nightmares of demons. This was not normal. Odd tummy pain began to start up in Taylor. Something was really off in the home, I could tell. It seemed to come to a head after I miscarried the twins. Now that I realized there was an open door of sin that satan was using to get to us through Sam, I asked Pastor Karen if there was anything I could do about it. Could I somehow repent for Sam's sin? I explained that we'd talked about anger over the years, and Sam would try to change, but I sensed he didn't see the gravity of it. Was there anything else I could do? She brought me to this verse:

> *If anyone observes a fellow believer habitually sinning in a way that doesn't lead to death, you should keep interceding in prayer that God will give that person life* (1 John 5:16a TPT).

Using the above verse, I repented to the Lord right away for Sam's sin and then asked Jesus to help him see it as well, to repent, and change. Within twenty-four hours or so the demonic dreams and odd tummy pain stopped. It was astonishing how fast the change took place. There was such a sweetness in our home. Then I began to pray the following verses over Sam daily. I didn't go to Sam about the anger, I went to Holy Spirit, and asked *Holy Spirit* to reveal it to Sam:

> *[I always pray] that the God of our Lord Jesus Christ, the Father of glory, may grant you a spirit of wisdom and of revelation [that gives you a deep and personal and intimate insight] into the true knowledge of Him [for we know the Father through the Son]. And [I pray] that the eyes of your heart [the very center and core of your being] may be enlightened [flooded with light by the Holy Spirit], so that you will know and cherish the hope [the divine guarantee, the confident expectation] to which He has called you, the riches of His glorious inheritance in the saints*

(God's people), and [so that you will begin to know] what
the immeasurable and unlimited and surpassing greatness
of His [active, spiritual] power is in us who believe. These
are in accordance with the working of His mighty strength
(Ephesians 1:17–19 AMP).

Within in a couple of weeks, the Holy Spirit answered my prayers. Sam realized the gravity of anger and rage in his life and completely repented to the Lord. The peace that flowed afterward was so soothing and complete. Sam is so gentle spirited now, and calm. To this day, the house is peaceful overall. If any little bit of anger comes up, I see Sam quickly repent to us and to the Lord. Glory to God!

Further Cleansing

In addition, earlier that spring and summer, the Lord showed us to cleanse our home of things related to magic, witchcraft, spells, witches, potions, curses, and death. He highlighted certain things to get rid of, including: Disney, Minecraft, Pokémon, Starbucks, and other objects or related toys. We obeyed as He was calling us to a higher level of intimacy and friendship.

Jesus hates sin and asks His believers to be called out and separate from the world. We must be full of salt and light (Matthew 5:13-16) to truly affect the people around us with God's love. We cannot have any sin in the camp. I say "in the camp" because there is a story in the Book of Joshua where one of the Israelites chose to disobey God's orders and instead sinned. He brought sin into the camp of Israel. His sin ultimately negatively affected himself, his family, and many other families of Israel (Joshua 7).

Therefore "Come out from among them and be separate, says the Lord. Do not touch what is unclean, and I will receive you (2 Corinthians 6:17).

Just to be *very* clear, I do not think all miscarriages are caused by satan or are due to unconfessed sin. For us, however, I believe it was, and to this day, I thank God for setting us free.

Then Jesus said to those Jews who believed Him, "If you abide in My word, you are My disciples indeed. And you shall know the truth, and the truth shall make you free" (John 8:31–32).

Side Note: Please reflect on your life and the lives of your family members. Learn from us. If you see repetitive, unconfessed sin in your life or theirs, please repent. If for them, then keep diligently praying that they will see it and repent as well.

Chapter 12

Cross-Country Move by Faith

The fall of 2021 brought much change to our family. As many of you were probably going through hard times with covid, it affected us as well. Because air traffic is part of the federal government, when the mandate came out for all federal employees to take the shot, we began to pray steadily for wisdom. Sam was still an air traffic controller and the sole provider for our family. At that time, the shot had not been tested much, and we heard many bad things about it. There was no peace in our hearts for Sam to take the shot to keep his job. We kept praying. As Mr. Biden began asking for proof of compliance by a specific date for all federal employees, things got very real. Living in California on one income is a little tricky because of how expensive things are. We both still had peace for me to stay home and continue homeschooling the kids. Reality sank in though as we began considering leaving the FAA, as we realized we'd probably have to leave California as well, to substantially lower our cost of living and quickly. We continued to pray and seek the Lord heavily for wisdom.

On my walk one afternoon, the Lord dropped into my spirit, "Sell high!" There was urgency in His voice. Financial investing is not my strong suit, and I don't say things like that. My spirit knew this direction was coming from the Lord. After explaining to Sam what Holy

Spirit told me and that it felt urgent, he agreed. Sam loves to invest, and was already considering selling our California home in order to move us out of state if it came to that. He understood what Holy Spirit was saying. Based on the market at the time, we could make a good profit from our home.

Sam and I didn't have any further direction from the Lord as to *where* we were going, just that He wanted us to sell the home, which meant we were going *somewhere*. This took a lot of faith because we loved our neighbors and church family, but we had been praying for wisdom regarding Sam's job and the mandate. Selling the house felt related somehow.

Hating instability though, I asked the Lord in my quiet time, "Where are we going, Lord? I'm willing to obey, but how can you ask us to leave our friends, family, and home and not tell us where we are going?" I was getting a little *too* big for my britches, getting a little attitude with the Almighty (not a good idea). He was ever so patient; I felt the Lord just chuckle. He was quiet. I became a little more indigent. "Lord, when have you *ever* done this to anyone in the Bible before?" I felt if I could prove my point, this being *way* too much to ask of someone (to sell our home, pack, leave family and friends, and still not know where we were going) that He may break and tell me our destination. The Spirit of the Lord answered matter-of-factly, "Abraham." As I heard His answer, I also felt Him smile with satisfaction. I looked it up quickly, and sure enough, God was right. God is always right.

> Now the LORD had said to Abram: "Get out of your country, from your family and from your father's house, to a land that I will show you (Genesis 12:1).

For some reason, if I see something in Scripture, it helps me tremendously. If Abraham didn't know where he was going, and he still obeyed God, then I could too. Shortly after that, to confirm things for Sam and I, the Lord gave two people at our church words of knowledge about our move; both resonated with us and encouraged us. They were not details on the destination, just confirming words that God wanted us to move and to go quickly. We began putting feet to our faith, sold our goats, and cleaned up the barns quickly. We ordered moving PODS and began filling them.

> *But someone will say, "You have faith, and I have works."*
> *Show me your faith without your works, and I will show*
> *you my faith by my works* (James 2:18).

We kept praying for direction and timing. With the compliance date drawing near, so much was up in the air. We prayed diligently. Earlier Sam had put in a letter of request for exemption not to take the shot, but we hadn't heard back from HR and weren't sure we would before the compliance deadline. Was this a local move? A long distance move?

We listed our house by faith, and folks began viewing it. We were living bear minimum now; the move was getting very real. We kept asking the Lord what the next step was. One of the PODs was in local storage now, and the other was still in our driveway getting packed. "Where do we ship the moving PODs, Lord? Where do we ship Sam's truck? Where do we point the van and begin driving, Lord?" In answer to our torrent of questions, the Lord gave us our next step.

> *Your word is a lamp to my feet and a light to my path*
> (Psalms 119:105).

The Lord reminded my husband about some rental properties he recently purchased in North Carolina. They were super run-down and fully rented out (from the previous owner). Sam had planned to remodel each duplex over time and then rent them out for a premium. He hadn't begun any of this work yet but had planned to do it long distance through a team of people in North Carolina. Wouldn't you know it, about this time, one of the tenants reached out to Sam, telling him she planned to move out in about ten days. She lived in one side of one of the duplexes. Sam looked at me and said something like, "It's a two-bedroom, and it needs work, but it'll be available in about ten days. What do you think, Babe?" I'll be honest, my fleshly side knew how run-down the rentals were, and a two-bedroom? Well, let's just say I had to die to myself that day. My mature side said something like, "It looks like the Lord is opening a door, doesn't it?"

Sam prayed and prayed about leaving the FAA; he'd worked for the federal government for years, and enjoyed air traffic. But in the end, we had no peace about Sam taking the shot to keep his job. Not having peace *was* the answer, and North Carolina *was* the direction. We understood the Lord was leading us step by step away from the FAA and out of California. We obeyed.

Peace flooded our souls as we packed the minivan. We said our goodbyes to our beloved neighbors, friends, and family and began our cross-country trip to North Carolina. With a couple of states under our belt, we received a phone call from the realtor that there was a family wanting to buy our California home. We quickly entered escrow at full price. This huge provision was yet another confirmation that God was leading us and providing for us.

Homeschooling on the road was stretching at times, but we figured it out. We began having fun with it too—stopping off at educational places along the way (the Grand Canyon, a fort, a cavern). We were totally living by faith. This was a whole new level of obedience and trust for us: no major income, some savings in the bank, and living out of our van. We were not afraid, though; we knew God was leading us. Our destination, although not certain it would be long-term, was a small, run-down duplex in North Carolina.

For all who are allowing themselves to be led by the Spirit of God are sons of God (Romans 8:14 AMP).

Road Trip!

The Grand Canyon

Fantastic Caverns

North Carolina

To give a comparison, our home back in California was nice but humble. It was a simple three-bed, 1,400-square-foot home. Back then, I thought that was a little snug, but doable. Boy, did I have a lot to learn! As we pulled up to the duplex in North Carolina, I realized just how *small* a two-bed, 650-square-foot home could be. It was incredibly small and run-down, but we were thankful to have a home.

With one side of the duplex being vacant "just in time," we knew the Lord was providing for us. We didn't feel led to rent or buy anywhere else. We felt He wanted us there. Since we already owned the duplex, and Sam was in between jobs, it made total sense. Later we found He had ministry work for us in the community as well. God is always busy doing multiple things behind the scenes. He is so good!

With some of the income we made on the sale of our California home, Sam began remodeling and improving the other rentals we had in North Carolina. After school, I would let Zachariah and Taylor help him in the afternoons. I'd also dive in when I could and help out with whatever Sam needed: demo work, yard work, water department hook-up, bills, and so on. It was fun to see us all working toward a common goal, and it was wonderful being together with Sam more often. He had driven to work for years, so to have him around the house, coming and going as he went to Lowe's or met with trades, was great! God was physically drawing us together with the two-bedroom and emotionally drawing us together as our family learned to work as a team.

Chapter 13

Living on a Budget and Job Instability

In this season of our lives, the Lord taught us how to live on a budget. We were mainly living off our savings until Sam secured a local job. We learned the difference between our needs and our wants. At some point as we were all adjusting, I think it was Julia who asked if we could go to Olive Garden or some restaurant like that. I actually laughed out loud without meaning to hurt her feelings. We used to go often to restaurants like that in California. I don't say this pridefully; looking back, I wish we hadn't. We could have saved money over the years had we eaten at home more often. Anyway, I told her something like, "Honey, we're not exactly Olive Garden people anymore; we're more like Burger King *with* a coupon people now." She didn't get it, but Sam and I chuckled. It was true. Things like the expensive shampoo and conditioner I ordered every other month for years were now being called into question. Sam asked if the cost could start coming out of my allowance, which he also had to lower during this season. He even lowered the kids' allowance. We were all feeling the crunch and trusting God in this transition.

We often spoke with the children about how we were trusting the Lord to provide for us. We knew Sam would get his bearings and find local work, but in the meantime, we wanted to be frugal and careful with our savings. Holy Spirit even taught me how to homeschool in a very small space with bare minimum things. It was humbling but so good for us. The children began to share more and became better peacemakers as they all bunked up in one room. God even taught me how to be a better cook in a small, old kitchen, as eating out was not in the budget for the most part.

As we settled in, we began meeting the neighbors. There were *so* many kids! Our kids hit it off with them quickly and enjoyed playing together often. We were enjoying how fresh and green our surroundings were as well. We were really falling in love with North Carolina.

Gingerbread Houses with the Neighborhood Kids

Bonfire Night with the Neighborhood Kids

New Pregnancy

During all of this adjusting, the Lord began fanning the flame in my heart for another baby. Although we'd been through so much on that front, I couldn't shake the fact that I still believed God wanted to increase our family size. The Lord is so gentle, especially when you need it. He began to quietly show me certain number sets everywhere. I kept seeing 111 everywhere or 1:11 on the clock.

Side Note: I have found that when the Lord shows you a repeat number, one that just keeps jumping out to you everywhere (the clock, license plates, street signs, and so on), that it's an invitation from Him. He wants to tell you something if you're willing to search it out. Sometimes it means a chapter and verse, other times it means a date or something else; just ask Holy Spirit, and He will tell you.

This time, I believe God was showing me Bible verses. I knew the popular Hebrews verse, but my sister Sally had recently sent me a verse in Deuteronomy as well. I began declaring both of these verses out loud over our family often and agreeing with God for more children.

> *Now faith is the substance of things hoped for, the evidence of things not seen* (Hebrews 11:1).

> *May the Lord God of your fathers make you a thousand times more numerous than you are, and bless you as He has promised you!* (Deuteronomy 1:11)

We became pregnant in December of 2021. After everything we'd been through, I was a bit nervous as you can imagine, but right away, the Lord gave me a phrase from an old hymn of victory to recite, which I did again and again. I kept declaring the Lord's victory and God's faithfulness throughout the first trimester, and would often put my hands on my tummy and declare the blood of Jesus over the baby (as a protection). We all prayed diligently for the baby and a good, healthy pregnancy. We kept reviewing our lives often for any sin. If anything came up, we quickly repented. We were especially careful with our words and spoke good things over ourselves and over the baby.

Why watch your words, you may wonder? It simply goes back to us being made in God's image, and what we say is powerful.

You will declare a thing, and it will be established for you;
so light will shine on your ways (Job 22:28).

Death and life are in the power of the tongue, and those
who love it will eat its fruit (Proverbs 18:21).

That first trimester was a complete faith walk with Jesus. He never left my side. He was *right* there with me, patiently reassuring me the whole way. Multiple times a day, I would hear Him whisper to me, "All is well." "You are fine." "Everything is fine." He also gave me a couple of dreams during this time that showed the baby being healthy in my womb. In one dream, I even saw myself going into labor about full-term. Thank you, Jesus! Deep parts of my soul began to heal, and I began to really enjoy the pregnancy. We were out of the first trimester now, and my tummy grew and grew. The strong nausea faded gently, normally, and baby kicks began. My heart soared.

Tight Quarters

Earlier in 2022, we purchased two Maltese puppies. Taylor *loves* dogs, and had been asking for a dog for a while. Choosing a dog was a little tricky though, because we were (and still are) praying to receive healing from the Lord for Zachariah, Taylor, and Sam of pet allergies. Since the Maltese is hypoallergenic, we decided on this breed. They were quite a bit of work to potty train but so very precious. We love them very much. However, with the kids, puppies, puppy crates/toys/food, and my tummy growing, it seemed the duplex walls were shrinking by the minute. When the couple across from us moved out of their side of the duplex, Sam opened up a wall to the other side, which gave us more space. It was not ideal, but it worked for a while and was a blessing.

Kids & Pups

Friendships with some of the neighbors began to really blossom. We often had their kids over for pizza, crafts, or just to play. After a while, the Lord put it on my heart to start a neighborhood Bible study. We did, and it was wonderful. Two of the kids got saved, and three prayed to receive the baptism of the Holy Spirit. I love blessing and helping children and telling them how much God loves them. My heart was so full of joy.

At this point, Sam had begun work as a loan originator. Although the pay was much less than he used to make in California, it helped. He took all the classes and was doing well, but the hours (eleven to thirteen-hour days) and stress of the job were taking a toll on his overall health. We prayed about it together and decided it wasn't a good fit.

He gave his notice, and we kept trusting the Lord and living frugally. We prayed the Lord would provide other work for Sam.

Around that time, the FAA dropped the mandate for the shot. We thought and prayed about Sam reapplying but to an air traffic facility locally. We had peace about Sam reapplying, and we began the very *long* wait to hear back from the FAA. During the wait, I had a dream that the FAA did indeed re-hire Sam and that his start date would be the end of May. This gave us such hope and excitement. We agreed with this dream by faith, knowing it was from the Lord. He was showing us a flash of what could be our future, hoping we'd agree with Him. We agreed, prayed for, and declared out loud often that Sam would work for the FAA again. With a growing family, the income and insurance would be very helpful.

Side Note: Please pay attention to your dreams; we see God using them often to guide us, confirm things in our lives, or warn us of what satan is up to.

Chapter 14

Another Diagnosis and More Angels

During the first ultrasound appointment for the baby, I couldn't stop smiling. His heartbeat was so strong and beautiful. They estimated his due date to be mid-September. Although thrilled, after I went home, I began to overanalyze one of the fuzzy ultrasound pictures they gave me. Something didn't quite look right on the picture, and I began to fear that something was wrong with the baby.

Around the twenty-week ultrasound, the doctor told me there appeared to be something wrong with the baby's health. He diagnosed him with probably having trisomy 18. He saw three signs of it. The doctor advised that if the baby did indeed have this, he would probably not live long and if he did live, he would need around-the-clock care. He asked me to come back in four weeks for a follow-up appointment.

That was definitely not the kind of news I was hoping to hear that day. It all seemed too familiar, a life-threatening diagnosis for one of our children. With a heavy sigh, I just fell back on my training. I remembered not siding with the doctors when Julia was diagnosed, and I wasn't going to side with this new doctor now. I wasn't in denial of what the doctor said, but I wasn't going to agree or accept what he said as truth either. This diagnosis would simply have to change because the truth is the baby was healed by Jesus' stripes. Even in the parking lot,

I remember saying out loud something like, "Lord, I know this isn't going to be our reality. I know this baby is healed by your stripes. I do not accept this diagnosis." I came home and immediately told Sam. We prayed together for healing over the baby. We'd seen God work miracles in our lives before with my thyroid, with Julia, against fevers, and other sicknesses. We knew God's character and His love for us.

The next morning, I came before the Lord for some one-on-one direction. He explained to me that by fearing for so long (it had been about a month) that something was wrong with the baby, the enemy was able to make it so. He said something about fear being a subtle sin and hard to detect. He was right; I didn't realize fear had been lingering in my heart for a month without repenting. I humbly asked the Lord to forgive me and to heal the baby. He seemed full of joy at my faith. He responded, "Yes, of course, and the healing won't take long." He mentioned a few months, and the healing would manifest. He encouraged me not to doubt and just believe.

> As soon as Jesus heard the word that was spoken, He said
> to the ruler of the synagogue, "Do not be afraid; only
> believe" (Mark 5:36).

Over the next couple of weeks, the Lord graciously gave me two similar dreams of the baby being made whole in my womb, completely healed, and it manifesting on the ultrasound monitor before I even gave birth.

Side Note: Whenever you receive two dreams or two signs of some kind from the Lord, please pay close attention. It's my understanding that whatever it is, it has been established

in heaven. Like Pharaoh's dream that Joseph interpreted (Genesis 41).

One night, during those two weeks, I woke with a very warm sensation all over my uterus. It startled me at first and lasted about an hour. I asked the Lord what was going on. The impression was, "The angels are here answering your prayer for the baby's healing." In the morning, as I woke fully, it sank in that the baby was healed! I was ridiculously excited and kept thanking and praising God.

Although the doctor in North Carolina wanted me to come back for a follow-up ultra sound four weeks later, we didn't have insurance anymore. Things were tight, and we didn't feel led to pay out-of-pocket for an ultrasound and my blood work. We trusted the Lord had healed the baby, and we would wait for an ultrasound later when God provided insurance or cash. It was difficult for me to cancel the appointment because I desperately wanted to see for myself the miracle manifest on the monitor, but we had peace to wait.

Chapter 15

The "Bug House" and Answered Prayer

I t was definitely a challenging season living in the duplex, and although having the whole duplex was helpful, each room was still very tiny, and most of the new side was used to store tools, drywall, a cement mixer, an air compressor, and so on. One bedroom became Zachariah's which was helpful, and the other became Sam's office while he was a loan originator. All that to say, things were still very cramped. I'm not complaining; I was extremely thankful to be in a warm, dry home, but when you're pregnant, you want to feel safe and settled. I felt neither as these were very old, run-down duplexes. Sam never intended for us to live in them. When he purchased them, he saw their condition and planned to always remodel after the tenants left and then get new renters.

The place was semi-clean when we moved in, but what I haven't mentioned yet was the bug infestation that was present. In addition, there had been smokers before us, so there were nicotine stains all over the counters, the tub, the sinks, and walls. With my pregnant nose added to the mix, the nausea was almost overwhelming. No matter how much I would scrub and clean, cockroaches and other black things would scurry here and there. For a bit, there was even a house mouse that actually stared me down one morning. I kept cleaning and cleaning, setting mouse traps, taking deep breaths outside, and praying hard for the Lord to provide a better place for us to live. At the same time, though, I knew we were impacting the neighborhood with love from Jesus, especially the children. We kept trusting the Lord for His timing, knowing we were furthering His kingdom while we were there. In addition, Sam and I knew he needed a good-paying job before we could really live anywhere better. As we waited to hear back from the FAA, Sam applied to various other jobs and had some phone interviews. Meanwhile, he stayed busy working on the other duplex remodel.

We were doing our best to stay on budget. I was cooking like crazy in the tiny kitchen, doing my best to keep things sanitary. We hardly *ever* ate out because we couldn't afford to. It was a good day if we had $1.50 ice cream cones from McDonalds.

Prayers continued, and then one afternoon in May, we came home from taking the kids to the park. Being pregnant, I usually brought up the rear while Sam would wait for me. The kids jumped out of the van and bounded into the house. As Sam and I followed, we began hearing scream after scream after, "*Oh no!*" Then all the kids re-appeared and ran back to us with frightened looks on their faces. We had no idea what was going on but figured it wasn't good. We'd been gone only an hour or two. What could possibly have happened inside the house?

Sam bravely went inside; I carefully peered behind him. I'd never seen anything like it in my life. There was what looked like a carpet of termites crawling and swarming all over our living room floor, couch, and window. Masses were everywhere. Some were even flying through the air. It appeared they had come up through the floor boards or ducts somehow, and were attempting to get outside. The couch was their on-ramp to the window and freedom it seemed.

I about lost it! I was done. I was *so* done. I couldn't take one more creepy-crawling thing living in our home. I said, "Sam, I'm done with this house. I'm so sorry, Honey, I can't stay here another day." Extremely rattled, I began packing our suitcases immediately. He agreed and began making hotel arrangements within minutes. At one point, Julia and I were in the kitchen, and she saw another cockroach scrambling in the drawer. She stood up and declared, "Mom, we need another house. This is a *bug* house." She stomped off disgusted. I couldn't have agreed with her more.

Big Digs

As we rolled into the parking lot of the local hotel that night, I quietly breathed a sigh of relief. We booked the hotel for a week to get our bearings and seek the Lord for wisdom. Before the week was up, the Lord answered us loud and clear. He reminded me of the FAA dream I had. It was the end of May, just like in the dream, and sure enough the FAA contacted us, offering Sam a position as an air traffic controller. They gave us a list of locations we could choose from across the country. We were thrilled, and with new income soon from the FAA, we had peace about not going back to the duplex. It was time to find something more suitable to live in. The Lord's communication and timing was perfect.

The FAA moves very slowly (usually), and we knew it would be a month or more until paperwork was processed. Because of this and the practical need to have a kitchen and a space for the kids to play safely while we waited, we knew we couldn't stay in the hotel forever. Sam thought it best to stay in an Airbnb (short-term-rental) for six weeks. He felt this amount of time would be enough for us to pray and decide the location, and also for the FAA to process the paperwork and assign a start date. His choice for an Airbnb was also to bless me with a safe, comfortable environment to live as I was about six months pregnant at the time. He knew I'd been stretched to my limits at the "Bug House."

Sam chose a home about twenty minutes away called Big Digs. It was huge and one of my best memories that summer. It had a local swimming pool, which the kids and I loved, and a fenced-in backyard for the dogs. In addition, it was clean, didn't smell, and had a huge kitchen. It was so refreshing.

The Federal Aviation Administration (FAA)

Sam has worked air traffic for years, starting in the military, and then for the FAA. Because of his background in mostly centers (high-level altitudes), the FAA only sent us a list of centers to choose from. We prayed over the list and felt led to choose the Atlanta Center. We were really falling in love with North Carolina and the southeast in general, but since there were no centers in North Carolina, we thought Georgia would be the next best state. Usually, the FAA will give you your first choice from the list, but not always. We assumed and prayed they'd give us our first choice (Atlanta Center), so we began looking for housing near Atlanta while we waited to hear back.

The FAA said yes to Atlanta Center and gave Sam a firm offer letter, including three options for start dates. The first date was July 17, 2022, then two more dates in August. This date jumped off the letter to me. I said, "Sam, you *have* to pick July 17! Do you see it?" He was puzzled. I reminded him of how July 17, 2019, was the day we found out Baby John was in heaven. Then July 17, 2021, was Baby Esther's due date (God wanting to redeem the date for us). Since Baby Esther was in heaven now as well, I saw how God was redeeming July 17 for us again but in a new way. Jesus loves to redeem dates, and His signature was all over this start date for Sam. As Sam realized the significance, he agreed and selected July 17, 2022.

While we waited for Sam's start date, we continued living in Big Digs, and making trips down to Georgia to look for housing. No matter how much we searched or what the realtor found for us, we couldn't seem to find a good fit. We didn't think we were being unreasonable in our search. Sam and I both had a short list of what we were hoping for. I was hoping for land so I could get some livestock and start gardening again. Sam wanted a pool and a big house. Nothing seemed to be right, though. *What are we missing,* I thought. We kept praying and searching for a house. We all became weary of looking at house after house, and time kept ticking by.

About a week before we were to leave Big Digs, the FAA called Sam and said, "What do you think about Jacksonville Center in Florida?" What a left turn! I was ecstatic. It was an automatic yes for me because over the past couple of years, I had been hearing all the amazing things God was doing in Florida and was quietly hoping we'd move there someday. Although I loved North Carolina and Georgia, and still do, I felt the Lord was doing wonderful things in Florida.

There is an air traffic center there in Jacksonville, but it was not on the original list, so this was a surprise to both of us. The FAA only gave us three hours to decide, hence my "usually" statement earlier. Wanting to be diligent with whatever God sends our way, we did what we could in three hours. There was no time to drive down and look around, so we called friends who used to live near there, and Sam quickly called an air traffic controller who had previously worked at the Jacksonville Center. This gentleman went on and on about the politics and how challenging the center was. He highly recommended that Sam *not* take the position. Ugh! I did my best to keep my mouth shut, but in my gut, I just *knew* we were supposed to say yes. I love Sam very much though and didn't want to force my way and push him to choose something he'd regret. In addition, as the wife, the Bible is clear that I am to submit to my husband (Ephesians 5:22), so I did.

Sam called the FAA back that night and thanked them but told them we'd stick with the Atlanta Center. My heart sank, and I couldn't shake the feeling that we'd just made a *huge* error. Not wanting to push Sam, I quietly took it to the Lord that night. It was a simple prayer, something like, "Lord, if we have somehow just made a huge mistake by turning down Jacksonville Center, please error-correct us as fast as you possibly can." I went to bed and slept peacefully, knowing I'd done everything I could.

The very next morning, the FAA called Sam back and rescinded the firm offer letter to the Atlanta Center. They said something like, "We need you at the Jacksonville Center. If you say no, you will be out of the running for this job posting." Essentially, they were saying, "Jacksonville or nothing." Sam and I couldn't help but laugh. He of course said yes. With time running out at the Airbnb, and me about seven months pregnant, Sam knew he needed to stabilize us quickly. He and I both saw this as God's divine intervention. God was still answering our prayers for provision, but was sending us exactly where He wanted us. We finally understood why housing wasn't working out for us in Georgia. I'm sure the Lord heard all of our prayers for housing in Georgia, but He knew the end game was Florida. He was protecting us and leading us.

Side Note: Sometimes "No" from the Lord is the best answer. He is faithful and true.

Shortly after that, we packed our bags, waved goodbye to Big Digs, and began the six-hour drive south to Jacksonville, Florida.

Chapter 16

Florida and Another Miracle

W
e stayed in a hotel near the Jacksonville Center for a few weeks as we began our search for housing in Florida. Day after day we toured homes. Nothing we were praying for seemed to open up. Finally, the Lord highlighted a descent rental home near Sam's facility. We wanted to buy, this was a rental. We wanted acreage, but this was in a planned community with tiny lots. We wanted a big house, this was medium size, but do-able. We didn't fully understand God's leading, but knew He was prompting us to choose *this* house. Physically and emotionally exhausted, we obeyed and signed the lease.

We had a home, at last. By then, Sam had begun work at the Jacksonville Center. We had a few precious weeks of summer left, so I began unpacking box after box as fast as I could. Being heavily pregnant, this wasn't easy. The children helped a lot, and so did Sam. We set up the classroom, the kitchen, and the children's bedrooms. I breathed a sigh of relief as the house began looking like a home. We were ready for school to start now and just about ready for Baby's arrival. We just needed to buy a crib and shop for baby clothes and diapers.

Along with Sam's new position came health insurance, and I was *very* excited to make a baby appointment. We had still been praying and believing all this time that Baby was healed. As soon as we were eligible, I made an appointment, but had to cancel and reschedule due to a hiccup in the paperwork at his facility (which I strongly felt was pushback from satan). Rescheduling for three more weeks out brought me to tears. Looking back, we experienced a lot of push back from satan while getting settled into Florida. satan or the regional demons in Jacksonville seemed *very* surprised and upset that we were there. However, knowing the Lord led us to Florida, we just kept standing our ground. I continued calling again and again to straighten out the insurance paperwork. In addition, as soon as we moved into the Florida home, within a week or two, all kinds of things began to happen. The AC stopped working, the dishwasher started acting up, the front door started sticking shut, the toilet handle broke, and the bathroom drawer handle fell off. Some people may say that's just a coincidence, but I could tell the enemy was very upset about us living in Florida. Later, I anointed the home with oil, and commanded anything from the darkness to leave in Jesus' name. Meantime, I kept calling maintenance, and we all did our best to be patient as they fixed or gave us new appliances for everything.

> *And we know that all things work together for good to those who love God, to those who are the called according to His purpose* (Romans 8:28).

All that to say, something was stirring in the supernatural. The lines had been drawn (light vs. dark). The Lord told me, "No more delay." There was urgency in His voice. The impression was, "Don't cancel your appointment again. Go with or without insurance to see the baby on the monitor." I obeyed, knowing He would provide.

The morning of the appointment, Sam had to work, so I found myself driving all three kids to the ultrasound appointment again (like back in 2019 to see a baby in my womb), but with great victory and triumph in my heart this time, believing I was about to see a miracle.

After about a two-hour wait, I kindly asked the nurse what was taking the doctor so long. I understood needing to wait thirty minutes, even an hour. But two? They said she was helping another mom labor and deliver currently, and that she would see me and the other patients waiting as soon as she could afterward. The nurse asked if I wanted to reschedule for another day. Remembering God's words about *no more delay*, we kept waiting. Another hour ticked by. The children were so hungry and fidgety by then. I did everything I could to hold it together with them in the tiny exam room. Finally, the doctor came in. I assumed since I was a new patient and especially because of the previous diagnoses, she would want to see the baby on the ultrasound. No, she didn't. She was just planning to speak with me about everything and measure the baby's growth. The Lord's words about *no more delay* came up again into my spirit. Exhausted and frustrated with all the push back from the enemy, I begged, "Please, Ma'am, have you read my chart? We have been praying for a miracle, and I believe the Lord has performed one already. We'd love to see the baby on the monitor today if there is any way possible." I had given her staff my chart earlier from the doctor's notes and diagnosis in North Carolina. She nodded that yes, she had read my chart. She smiled and stepped out for a moment. Understanding this was spiritual warfare, I quietly leaned over to the kids and said, "Everyone, start praying in tongues so the doctor will approve an ultrasound to see the baby today." We all started praying in tongues quietly and fervently.

Side Note: From personal experience, I have noticed praying and singing in tongues seems to bring things into this realm faster than praying in English.

Miracle on the Monitor

Moments later, the doctor stepped back in and said, "They're preparing the room for you." I was relieved and thanked the Lord. As the tech carefully looked all over my tummy, examining and measuring the baby, I did my best to stay calm and kept hearing the Lord say in my heart, "All is well." The children and I enjoyed hearing Baby's heartbeat.

Later, the doctor came in to discuss results. I told her how a few months back, my whole uterus was warm for an hour or so after we'd prayed for a miracle healing. She said, "When you said that just now, I got goose bumps all over!" She explained that she was a believer in Jesus as well. She double-checked pictures the tech had just taken and smiled, stating, "Everything looks great! The baby shows no sign of trisomy 18 or any other illness." She and I agreed that God had performed a miracle for our baby!

I couldn't stop smiling as I waddled out of the doctor's office that day with the children. Before we left the parking garage, I quickly text my mom, "All is well on earth as it is in heaven!"

In this manner, therefore, pray: Our Father in heaven, hallowed be Your name. Your kingdom come. Your will be done on earth as it is in heaven (Matthew 6:9–10).

Mom had been praying and believing right along with me that the miracle would manifest on the monitor. It did, just as Jesus told me it would, and just as He showed me by the double dream. Thank you, Lord. My heart was light and full of excitement. I was about thirty-five weeks along with a healthy baby!

Because we like to wait until the end of every pregnancy to find out whether a boy or girl, it's a little tricky to pre-buy clothes. Dad and Mom live in Michigan, and to include them as much as I could in the baby preparation, I asked Mom to pick out a boy and girl onesie as a take-home outfit. We had done this before, and it worked fine. You just use the one the baby is, and then return or give away the other outfit. She was thrilled and picked out two adorable baby outfits for my hospital bag.

Meanwhile, a kind group of women I'd gone to Bible study with in North Carolina wanted to bless me. They asked me to make a baby registry. I remember sitting down one evening and just relishing every choice online, carefully picking out baby clothes and other items we could use. By now, Julia was almost six years old, and we'd given most of our baby items away. To finally focus on the baby this way was such a blessing for me. Throughout the entire pregnancy I hadn't really been able to slow down, to feel safe, to prepare mentally and emotionally to be a mom again. I wanted to, and needed to, but most of the pregnancy had been rocky at best starting out in the tiny "Bug House," followed by the terrible diagnosis for the baby, then the constant prayers for healing all summer, hotel after hotel, the long search for housing, the move to Florida, finished by the whirlwind of unpacking, and insurance push back. Needless to say, I was exhausted and ready for life to slow down. I was so excited to be a new mom again and hold my precious sweet one and raise him or her to love Jesus. The following week I had another baby appointment. Baby was measuring great, and had a strong heartbeat. I was just over thirty-six weeks, and all was well.

Julia, Baby, and Me

Chapter 17

We Were So Close

The following afternoon, late in the day, as I played the piano, it dawned on me that I hadn't felt Baby kick for the past several hours. This baby was extremely active and very social. He was a light sleeper too; almost anything woke him. Later that evening, after tucking the kids into bed, I decided to mention it to Sam. He and I both tried to get Baby to wake up and come "talk to us." We'd usually get his attention by rubbing my belly, and he'd come right over and give us some kicks or wiggles... Nothing. I drank some ice water, hoping this would wake him up... Nothing. Our hearts started to sink rapidly. I said, "Honey, please take me in to see the doctor right now; something isn't right." He agreed, we grabbed the keys, and headed to the ER. After signing all the paperwork and ushering me back, it was about midnight. The on-call doctor brought in the ultrasound machine. I looked at her eyes pretty much the entire time, it was too difficult for me to look at the monitor. I had a feeling her eyes would reflect soon enough the news I was hoping *not* to hear. She pushed the wand here and there all over my tummy, concentrating on the monitor... Nothing. No movement. She finally put the wand away, looking at me with sympathy, she said, "I am so sorry. I'm not finding a heartbeat."

Oh, the utter sadness that swept over Sam and I in those moments. There are no words. We looked at one another, and I said, "We were so close. We were so close." Tears began to come as she wiped my tummy of the cream. The nurses helped me gather my things, and as they gave me their condolences, my training kicked in (my remembrance of what I had learned after all the other losses). Something came up from my spirit and out of my mouth. It was like I was listening, not the one speaking. I was saying how God was good and that I trusted Him. They seemed speechless in a good way as they gently hugged me. I'm sure that was all the Holy Spirit speaking through me because my heart was broken.

Prayer for Resurrection

They offered for me to deliver right then and there. We considered it, but it was so late at night. I was exhausted, and needed to talk with the Lord about it. We decided to go home and get a good night's rest. The idea of praying for resurrection wasn't foreign. It just wasn't where I wanted to be. I was exhausted on all fronts. I *just* wanted a healthy, live baby. We'd been trying for another baby for years. I was so emotionally drained from losing them. This was the fifth baby in a row we had lost. Part of me wanted to pray for resurrection, but I wasn't sure I was up for it, especially after the year we'd just had. And to ask our friends to join us again—well, hardly anyone asks you to pray for resurrection once, right? How about praying for it twice? Although exhausted physically, mentally, and emotionally, we loved the child, and of course we saw in Scripture that Jesus asks believers to raise the dead. So we attempted to obey.

And as you go, preach, saying, "The kingdom of heaven is at hand." Heal the sick, cleanse the lepers, raise the dead, cast out demons. Freely you have received, freely give (Matthew 10:7–8).

It all seems like a blur now, but I remember texting family and friends in tears that night, asking them to pray for resurrection – to pray God would miraculously bring the baby back to life. I had *just* seen the doctor the day before, and all was well. What happened? The baby was healed. God had proven that through the ultrasound the week before, and the doctor confirmed it. I realized then why the urgency in God's voice when He told me, "No more delay." I believe He knew what was coming, and He didn't want me to think the baby died of a foul disease. He wanted me to know without a doubt that He healed the child, and for it to show on the monitor.

We began to fervently pray for resurrection, for God to start the baby's heart again and make him or her whole. We asked our friends who *really* loved Jesus, true friends of God, to join us. The doctor called the next day or two and told me she would give me a week. She knew we were praying for a miracle but was concerned for my health, as many others were. This wasn't a miscarriage; this baby was practically full-term. I would have to labor and deliver now, whether the baby came back to life or not.

The days passed slowly as we continued to pray, still no movement. My body and emotions began tapping out. About four days into the week of praying, my body naturally went into labor. I labored through the night and got the family ready in the morning. We all piled into the van. Sam dropped me off at the hospital to deliver the baby, and he took the children elsewhere to wait. We were so new to Florida that we didn't know or trust anyone to watch the children for us. I longed to have Sam by my side but knew he needed to be with the children. The Lord's presence was with me though, steady and sure. In addition, I could sense the prayer support of many friends and family members.

The Delivery

Knowing our situation, the nurses admitted me quickly, and I labored back and forth in the room as long as I could, walking and squatting into the contractions. Tears streaming down my face, I sang praises to the Lord quietly and pleaded with Him to perform a miracle. It was the fastest and most intense labor and delivery I'd ever had. As the doctor examined the baby's lifeless body, she found the umbilical cord wrapped one time around the baby's neck. She believed that to be the cause of his death.

He was a boy. He was seven pounds, nineteen inches long. We named him James Frederick Lopez. One of the nurses kindly dressed him in the boy take-home outfit my mother sent. They allowed me to snuggle him. I kissed his precious head and hands. As I cradled him in my arms, I sobbed quietly. The kids and Sam arrived about then. We all did our best to hold it together. We laid hands for healing and for resurrection again and again. We believed beyond belief that James was coming back to life at any moment.

As his color began to fade, and his body started to cool off, I kept hearing in my spirit a gentle voice saying, "Let go. Let go." I knew it was Holy Spirit; He was answering us. I just didn't like the answer. With tears of deep sorrow and pain, I slowly handed James' lifeless body to the nurse. She gently and carefully placed him in the bassinet near my bed. The physical side of things began to catch up with me. Laboring, delivering a baby, hardly eating for the past twenty-four hours, praying for resurrection from the dead, weeping and weeping, my heart breaking, I desperately needed to rest.

I was ready to go home and sleep, but per Florida state law, you cannot leave a baby at the hospital who has died without picking a funeral home first. We planned to pick one; we just wanted to wait until morning, but they would not allow that. So the trauma continued. How do you pick a funeral home? I had no idea. The nurse gave me a list they used in the past for families like ours. I quickly found one, and made arrangements. Then I signed the necessary paperwork for my hospital release, and they brought in a wheelchair. The stream of tears would not stop. As I lovingly looked at our baby son's body for the last time, I placed my hand on his head, and out of my spirit came, "The Lord bless you and keep you, the Lord make his face to shine upon you, and give you peace" (Numbers 6).

Sam took the girls down to get the van and Zachariah stayed behind to be with me. Before we left the room, the nurse handed me a small, white box of little mementos she'd collected for me (James' fingerprints, footprints, his hat, a poem). I held it in my lap quietly as she wheeled me to the hospital exit, thinking how empty my arms felt. Normally, you leave the hospital snuggling your new baby as they wheel you down to your vehicle. This time I was leaving what felt like my baby behind. I know it was just his body, and the *real* James was in heaven…but it was still so hard. Instead of a warm, precious baby, I was holding a small, cold box… so unnatural. So empty. So confusing.

The Cemetery

The following days felt upside down and filled with sorrow. A day or two after delivery, my milk came in. My body and mind still wanted to nurse my infant son, but I couldn't. He was in heaven. There was physical pain with each letdown, and as I tried to stop the flow, more pain would come emotionally. I didn't want to stop the flow; I wanted to nurse my son. In those first couple weeks, I would often look at the ceiling and whisper, "Where did you go, sweet James . . . where did you go?" I knew exactly where he went, but heaven seemed so far away. My mind and body were still aching to hold him... to nurse him.

The Lord sent Mom down from Michigan to help us almost immediately, and what a blessing she was. She is an amazing cook and such a fun Grandma to the kids. Her love was *just* what we needed. The kids really, really needed some fun. They'd been watching me cry for a while now. They missed James too, but it's different for children somehow.

Mom took them shopping, to the park, and played with them. They loved every minute. We could feel God hugging us from heaven with her presence. Meanwhile, Sam was right by my side. The FAA was generous about time off, especially knowing the situation. He and I would talk together, pray together, and cry together. When it came time to pick the casket, I about lost it. None of them seemed right. It was honestly traumatizing (for me) just to look at baby caskets. I love children so dearly. We weren't even supposed to be shopping for caskets. I thought we were *supposed* to be shopping for a crib, diapers, and baby clothes. *God, please help us! What happened?*

We decided on what's called a green cemetery. This is where the funeral home simply wraps your loved one's body in a blanket, and you lay them in the earth – no casket, no headstone, just a simple marker. As the day drew near for the funeral, Mom, Sam, and I had a conversation. We all wanted to pray for resurrection one more time at the cemetery just in case we heard God wrong, just in case.

The day of the funeral arrived. That morning, our daughter Taylor saw an angel in the front yard. She said he was very bright and white, and his hair was short and blond. We were so excited about this, hoping perhaps the Lord had sent a resurrection angel to help us.

It was a long, ninety-minute drive to the cemetery. When we arrived, the funeral director brought James' wrapped body to us. Sam carried him to the site. We asked her and the cemetery gentleman to give us some time alone. They agreed and stepped back a distance. We all prayed and prayed for the Lord to raise James from the dead. We commanded him to come back in Jesus' name. It was about eleven days after his death, so we knew this would be an outright miracle, but we had faith for it. Nothing happened. We prayed some more. Then I heard the Holy Spirit gently saying again, "Let go." I finally understood; this was final. It was time to obey and to let go.

It felt like time stood still as I rocked James' body for what I knew would be the last time (on earth). I sang him a goodnight lullaby and then slowly, reluctantly, handed his precious body over to Sam. Sam carefully stood up and moved to the hole they had dug for him. He knelt down and gently laid James' body in the grave. Earlier, I knitted James a blanket, and instead of taking him home in it, I was now tucking him in with it for the first and the last time all at once. As the cemetery gentleman and Sam began to cover James' small body with dirt, Mom and I stood nearby. We were crying and holding hands, trusting God. The children stood next to us. They did well processing what was happening and trying to be quiet and respectful.

As the last bit of dirt was placed on top, we all stood together and sang a song of praise to the Lord. We felt it was right to give God praise. It's so important to praise God in the good times and in the bad times. He is always good and worthy of our praise. Mom and I and the girls laid flowers on top of James' grave, then we all began the quiet walk back through the cemetery field to our van.

It felt like the world should have stopped spinning. How would I ever come back from this? My heart was rocked and full of sorrow. As I closed the van door and sank into the seat, I was quickly jerked back into reality when Julia shouted from the back of the van, "I'm hungry, Momma!" The other kids chimed in, "Me too, me too." I knew right then the world wasn't going to stop, and neither could I.

Chapter 18

Learning to Have Grace

We took about a week of school off so I could physically rest without adding homeschool to the mix. As I rested, Mom kept blessing us with wonderful home-cooked meals, a clean house, and spent lots of time with the kids. Meanwhile, the Lord kept downloading dream after dream to Sam, the kids, and I. He was communicating His love and direction to us. I appreciated every drop of insight and took many notes in my journal.

Kids are kids, though, and our three on earth are no exception. After about a week of relaxing with Grandma, video games, and popcorn, they began to get a little squirrely. We had to assimilate some kind of schedule soon. Mom and I teamed up and slowly began teaching the kids their school lessons. Mom taught Julia, and I taught the older kids for a couple of hours each day. This helped quite a bit and began to stretch me to get out of bed more often. Meanwhile, many of our friends and family kept sending cards, flowers, meals, and prayers. The Lord was engulfing us with His love.

Almost every day Mom, Sam, and I would sit and talk through our feelings and encourage one another to keep loving and trusting God no matter the pain. Some days I felt like I made progress, while other days I felt like I crashed and burned because there were so many raw emotions. I remember researching things online like how to dry up breast milk, and (about a month later) how soon can you exercise after giving birth? At times the answers would sting, even though the article writers meant no harm. I would find myself getting hurt and offended at their answers. Things like, "Although you can dry up your breast milk, we highly recommend breast feeding your baby instead of formula feeding. It's better for you *and* the baby." I thought, *I absolutely agree – but my baby is in heaven. I don't have the option to breast feed him.* There were other answers like, "One great tip for losing weight after giving birth is to push the pram (stroller). It's great resistance, and will add to the loss of calories." Again, just an innocent article writer, but hot anger welled up inside me as I thought, *I would LOVE to push the pram, but I can't because my baby is in heaven.*

Other things began to crop up as well – innocent jokes, that I probably once laughed at, now hurt if I heard them in a movie or in other conversation:

"Honey – how was your day?"

"Well, I kept all the kids alive, so that's a plus."

Or even meeting a new mom at the park became complicated:

"Nice to meet you, how many kids do you have?"

Normally I'd just rattle off, "Three, and you?" But after Baby John moved to heaven, and as the losses continued, there became this gray area... *Is this gal really interested in my story? Do I list all the kids or just mention the ones on earth...? Wait, is it lying if I don't mention the ones in heaven...?*

My life is just different now. Not as cut-and-dry. It's less care free. It feels like Sam and I have gained access to a club we never wanted to be part of...still, members none-the-less. A club of parents who have also lost a baby or a child. It's a sober-minded club. It's a mature group of people who realize how fleeting life can be. Who realize things don't always go as planned. Who realize a pregnancy doesn't always equal a live baby. Who count their blessings again and again, and cherish life like never before.

To that end, I had some learning to do about having grace with others who were *not* in the club. About a month after James moved to heaven, we were attending church. Still very new to the area, we didn't know many people there, and they didn't know us or our story yet either. A young mom was up front welcoming everyone before the service began. She was talking about her three-month-old baby, and how challenging her life was currently with nursing him and getting him to burp properly. She was somehow tying it into a life-lesson for the congregation, but I had to fight back tears and anger. Her words just felt so insensitive, so naive. I thought, *At least your baby is alive so he can burp. Mine is in heaven. Why are you carrying on like this?*

I had a lot to learn. The Lord needed to have me dig deep, to forgive and not to be offended by these comments. He needed me to love all these well-meaning people in person or who wrote articles. Nothing was intentionally aimed at me to hurt me. We had just experienced something in life that most others had not. I remember being a new mom of Zachariah, of course this mother was concerned that her new baby was eating and burping properly. She seemed like a good mother, just navigating new waters. Thankfully, God kept working on my heart, maturing me.

> *I am the true Vine, and My Father is the vinedresser. Every branch in Me that does not bear fruit, He takes away; and every branch that continues to bear fruit, He [repeatedly]*

prunes, so that it will bear more fruit [even richer and finer fruit] (John 15:1-2 AMP).

As I kept trusting the Lord, and He kept healing me inside and out, I began to forgive and not be offended by anyone anymore. I began to love my neighbor as myself (Mark 12:31). As a practical application, as mothers and babies would pass me in the grocery store or while out taking a walk, the Holy Spirit guided me to pray a thanksgiving prayer over the child instead of tearing up or getting jealous or angry. As we passed each other, I would dig deep and say quietly, "Lord, thank you that *their* baby lived. Thank you that this family isn't grieving like we are. Please bless that baby and his family. Let him live a long life, and please help the whole family to come to know you as Savior if they do not know you already."

This simple prayer helped me immensely. I realized my heart becoming soft, accepting what had happened in our life, and also becoming full of grace and love towards others. In addition, from the unintentional hurt I experienced from others, I have become very aware of my thoughts and words towards others. The truth is, none of us knows the extent of what others have gone through in their lives (or are currently going through). Holy Spirit knows though, and if we yield to His guidance, He can lead us to be compassionate and sensitive towards others with our words and deeds.

> *However, when He, the Spirit of truth, has come, He will guide you into all truth; for He will not speak on His own authority, but whatever He hears He will speak; and He will tell you things to come* (John 16:13).

Blessed be the God and Father of our Lord Jesus Christ, the Father of mercies and God of all comfort, who comforts us in all our tribulation, that we may be able to comfort those who are in any trouble, with the comfort with which we ourselves are comforted by God (2 Corinthians 1:3-4).

Chapter 19

In This World You Will Have Trouble

Two to three weeks after the funeral, I began to ask God some hard questions. *What happened, God? Was it our fault somehow? Why is our sweet James in heaven with you?* We had so much peace in our home since the anger was gone; I thought we'd shut the door to further loss in the womb. There was *no* demonic dream or demonic scream as James passed. This was different; it wasn't even a miscarriage. This was an almost full-term baby I had carried, prayed for, and talked to for months. The emotional pain was very real. I guess I thought the spiritual warfare we had experienced over the years was more like a formula. If we kept sin out of our lives and obeyed God, then satan couldn't touch us, and God could bless us easily, right? To that point, I remember telling Sam one day about James' death, "We didn't sow for this, Honey. I'm so confused. How are we reaping this?"

> *Do not be deceived, God is not mocked; for whatever a man sows, that he will also reap* (Galatians 6:7).

Although this statement is true, there are many other factors at play in this fallen world that I was not considering. Yes, there are concepts in the Bible that if followed, can tremendously help avoid pain and sorrow, like you will reap what you sow (if you sin, there will be consequences). So don't sin. I understood all that, and I guess that had been my focus for years. What I hadn't been considering were all the trials and tribulation verses *also* mentioned in Scripture. There are many verses that mention strong believers in Christ reaping what they did *not* sow. This revelation was extremely hard for me to process.

> *It is through many tribulations and hardships that we must enter the kingdom of God* (Acts 14:22b AMP).

> *Yet if anyone suffers as a Christian, let him not be ashamed, but let him glorify God in this matter* (1 Peter 4:16).

The Lord reminded me of the parable of the wheat and the tares (Matthew 13), where an enemy sows tares among good wheat. The farmer then reaped what he did *not* sow. The impression was that we did not sow for James' death. This reaping of him being in heaven was not our fault. Then the Lord showed me the passage (John 9) where Jesus healed a man blind from birth. His disciples asked Him if it was the blind man's sin or the sin of his father that caused the blindness. Jesus answered that it was neither one but that the Father would get the glory in his healing. Again, Holy Spirit was showing us that it was not our fault but that God wanted us to glorify Him through it.

Later, Sam mentioned that about half way through the pregnancy, he had a dream about the baby dying by way of the umbilical cord. Surprised, I asked if he had prayed against it. He said, "Yes, absolutely. I rebuked satan and what I saw in the dream in Jesus' name and then prayed against it." Although very grateful Sam did something about it, this left me confused. If Sam took authority over what he saw in the dream, why did it still happen? Still going back to my formula thinking (1+1 *must* = 2), I asked one of my friends who loves Jesus. She said she felt Sam didn't pray it through. She felt James would still be alive today if we'd taken our authority over the devil properly. She kept mentioning this verse:

> *Behold, I give you the authority to trample on serpents*
> *and scorpions, and over all the power of the enemy, and*
> *nothing shall by any means hurt you* (Luke 10:19).

It felt like she was saying our pain and sorrow was our own fault. Another family who loves Jesus very much made a similar comment about a year earlier as we were going through loss back then, something about them noticing everything we were doing in life seemed to be failing. Like, what are you doing wrong? Why so many trials in your life?

The Lord led me to speak with another mom during this time who is a believer in Jesus and had lost many children in the womb as well. She mentioned a similar thing; a well-meaning believer in Christ told her if she'd been doing things correctly, she would still have the baby she (at the time) was miscarrying. To be clear, this woman miscarrying was not in sin or doing anything wrong.

Address to the Body of Christ

I'd like to lovingly speak to the body of Christ who may have spoken out of turn like this to a fellow believer in Christ. Words like this can *really* hurt someone. Please watch your words carefully. Unless you feel specifically sent by God to show a believer their error, like Nathan the prophet was sent to King David (2 Samuel 12), then please don't go. If God hasn't sent you, you might only be hurting the person further or possibly speaking incorrectly over their life, like Job's friends spoke incorrectly over Job (Job 42). Please seek the Lord carefully before giving advice or comments to a person who is already in such a vulnerable state of grief or pain. There are absolutely times for correction. The Bible is filled with guidance on how we should live our lives as believers, but we must rightly divide the Word of Truth. It's very easy to take one verse and become legalistic with it. Please seek the Holy Spirit diligently before correcting a member of the body of Christ. Study the Scriptures carefully. Be absolutely sure you have God's heart on the matter and are being sent by Him with love.

> *All Scripture is given by inspiration of God, and is profitable for doctrine, for reproof, for correction, for instruction in righteousness, that the man of God may be complete, thoroughly equipped for every good work* (2 Timothy 3:16-17).

> *Be diligent to present yourself approved to God, a worker who does not need to be ashamed, rightly dividing the word of truth* (2 Timothy 2:15).

To those of you who have been hurt by a member of the body of Christ, may I apologize to you on their behalf. I am so sorry for whatever they said or did that hurt you. The body of Christ is meant to be unified and full of love toward one another. As humans though, we all mess up from time to time. We must forgive each other. Speaking from experience, forgiveness will set you free from satan coming in and trying to start worse things in your life, like bitterness or resentment (all of which are demons, I believe). Please, if you can, as you can, forgive the person, and move on. Ask Holy Spirit to help you. You do not have to trust the person or ever speak to them again, but God *does* call you to forgive them.

Correction from Holy Spirit

> **Just because a believer is going through trials does not mean they are doing anything wrong.**

The Holy Spirit took care of the situation right away. He told me my friend's advice was not correct, and that neither was the family's comments a year or so ago. I have forgiven them all. He was showing me that not everything is a formula. Just because a believer is going through trials does not mean they are doing anything wrong.

> *I have told you these things, so that in Me you may have [perfect] peace. In the world you have tribulation and distress and suffering, but be courageous [be confident, be undaunted, be filled with joy]; I have overcome the world." [My conquest is accomplished, My victory abiding]* (John 16:33 AMP).

> *Yet if anyone suffers as a Christian, let him not be ashamed, but let him glorify God in this matter* (1 Peter 4:16).

God reminded me that He already told us James' death was not our fault. Then He led me to speak with a man and woman of God who love Him dearly. During our conversation, they were able to explain God's heart to me more clearly. Going back to what the woman spoke over us regarding the dream and she thinking Sam did not pray it through, the gentleman explained, "What would praying hard enough or praying it through to save James' life really look like? Ten minutes a day? Ten hours a day? How about twenty-four hours a day? Would that have been enough?" He was highlighting the legalism in this thought pattern, the formula style thinking: do everything right, take your authority over the devil properly and good things will happen. Jesus did everything right, and the Scripture says He was a man of sorrows and acquainted with grief (Isaiah 53:3).

I finally understood. After Sam had that dream, he prayed what he prayed as a believer in Christ; he took authority over satan the best way he knew how. Don't you think Jesus could have worked with Sam's prayer to save James' life? He certainly could have. Why He didn't was not clear to us, but that's when trusting our good heavenly Father comes in. The kingdom of heaven must be entered into as a little child, with childlike faith and trust. It's okay if we don't always understand – He gives us peace that *passes* our understanding as we trust and obey Him.

> But Jesus said, "Let the little children come to Me, and do not forbid them; for of such is the kingdom of heaven" (Matthew 19:14).

> And the peace of God, which surpasses all understanding, will guard your hearts and minds through Christ Jesus (Philippians 4:7).

Chapter 20

Count It All Joy

As the months passed by, I kept meditating on the fact that trials and tribulations can still come to the believer, and that we are to count them as joy because they mature us in our walk with the Lord.

> *My brethren, count it all joy when you fall into various trials, knowing that the testing of your faith produces patience. But let patience have its perfect work, that you may be perfect and complete, lacking nothing* (James 1:2-4).

As this realization sank in, I asked the Lord to show me in Scripture where other believers experienced trials and tribulations in their walk with the Lord. The Holy Spirit was happy to oblige; here are a few examples:

- Shadrach, Meshach, and Abednego were thrown into a furnace of fire because they chose to obey God and not bow down to an idol in worship (Daniel 3).

- Esther lost her parents and then had to leave her uncle as she was forced to marry a king whom she may or may not have loved. She then chose to put her own life in danger to save many Jews (Book of Esther).

- Zacharias and Elizabeth were barren for years, and yet God called them righteous (Luke 1:5–7).

- Paul was shipwrecked, bitten by a snake, beaten, left for dead, and many other things because he preached the gospel of Jesus Christ with love and boldness (Acts 28 and 2 Corinthians 11).

- Paul's thorn does not appear to be related to sin, but rather a messenger from satan sent to torment him (2 Corinthians 12:7–10).

- Jesus prophesied Peter would die a hard death for preaching the gospel (John 21).

- John the Baptist was imprisoned and died for preaching the gospel (Mark 6).

- **Even Jesus Himself was a man of sorrows and acquainted with grief (Isaiah 53:3).**

Understanding that all these saints and Jesus Himself suffered sorrow and went through grief at no fault of their own is comforting somehow. I am not alone. You are not alone in your sorrow and grief.

Reasons for Trials and Tribulations

Seeing all these testimonies in Scripture, and reflecting on our own life, the Lord began to highlight some reasons for trials and tribulations:

- Trials can come to anyone; some are caused by our own sin or the sin of others while others are not our fault at all (Galatians 6:7 and John 16:33).

- *Continued* trials and attacks from satan seem to follow the believers who are God's close friends, those who pose a threat to the kingdom of darkness (Life of Abraham, Moses, Paul, and others, also Revelation 3:15-16 seems to be related).

- Tests and trials can create deep compassion for others going through similar things (2 Corinthians 1:3-4).

- Glorifying God through tests and trials can mature the believer in Christ in a very deep way (Acts 16:22-30 and James 1:2-4).

- The trials and attacks happen often while the believers are preaching the gospel or spreading God's Word (Book of Acts).

- Miracles, signs, and wonders often follow the attacks and trials (The Gospels and Book of Acts).

- Trials seem to cause the gospel to be spread further (The whole New Testament really).

Although this information is not warm and fuzzy, it is packed full of hope and truth for the Kingdom of God. I am very honored to be about my Father's business, even if it includes trials and tribulations.

> *Beloved, do not think it strange concerning the fiery trial which is to try you, as though some strange thing happened to you; but rejoice to the extent that you partake of Christ's sufferings, that when His glory is revealed, you may also be glad with exceeding joy* (1 Peter 4:12–13).

> *Yet if anyone suffers as a Christian, let him not be ashamed, but let him glorify God in this matter* (1 Peter 4:16).

> *My brethren, count it all joy when you fall into various trials, knowing that the testing of your faith produces patience. But let patience have its perfect work, that you may be perfect and complete, lacking nothing* (James 1:2–4).

Raise the Dead vs. Let Go

As we close out our time together, I feel very led to share this last bit of insight regarding raising the dead. As the months passed by and our tears began to dry, a question started to quietly roll around in my spirit. Why would Jesus command us to raise the dead in Scripture (Mattew 10:8), but the Holy Spirit told us to let go? It seemed like an out-right contradiction. I'm sure many people over the years believing for resurrection from the dead have also wondered, *Why didn't it work?* As I pondered this question and reflected on both of our seasons of prayer for resurrection from the dead for our sons, John and James, something seemed to click inside my heart. I believe the Lord gave me the answer without me even formally asking Him. It was a simple verse, but filled with revelation:

> *For as many as are led by the Spirit of God, these are sons*
> *of God* (Romans 8:14).

The Father was showing me that as sons of God – we must be led by Holy Spirit all the time. Doing good things on our own or even doing good things we see in Scripture isn't necessarily wrong, but we may wear ourselves out or not be successful if we are not being led by the Spirit. Jesus was our role model on earth. He did nothing but that which the Father told Him to do. He was constantly being led by Holy Spirit to do God's will on earth, and He was constantly successful. As imitators of Christ, we too must be *constantly* led by Holy Spirit… every day, all day long.

> *Then Jesus answered and said to them, "Most assuredly,*
> *I say to you, the Son can do nothing of Himself, but what*
> *He sees the Father do; for whatever He does, the Son also*
> *does in like manner* (John 5:19).

> *Therefore become imitators of God [copy Him and follow*
> *His example], as well-beloved children [imitate their*
> *father];* (Ephesians 5:1 AMP).

Your ears shall hear a word behind you, saying, "This is the way, walk in it," whenever you turn to the right hand or whenever you turn to the left (Isaiah 30:21).

As I reflected on this revelation, I realized that although my heart desperately wanted both John and James to live, I do not remember Holy Spirit specifically leading us to raise the boys from the dead. I just thought we were automatically obeying God because of the imperative statement in Scripture, "Raise the dead" (Matthew 10:8). I'm not saying we were wrong to obey this command. I don't see the harm in believing and trying. But as I mature in the Lord, I want to grow and learn. A close friend of God gets God's heart. Hardly any strikeouts. Home-runs is what I'm after. The Bible never once said Jesus attempted to raise anyone from the dead. He just raised the dead when His Father led Him to. Jesus never *attempted* anything. He just *did* what the Father told Him to do on earth. I want to be like Jesus and have such a close relationship with the Father that I only do what He asks me to do.

The revelation kept flowing, "Don't you think Jesus wanted to raise His earthly father Joseph from the dead?" I thought, *Of course He would have, yes.* But Scripture doesn't seem to mention Joseph after Luke 2. I'm sure Jesus loved Joseph dearly, and yet His heavenly Father wasn't wanting (or asking) Jesus to raise Joseph from the dead. The verse in Isaiah 53:3 came to mind:

He is despised and rejected by men, a Man of sorrows and acquainted with grief. And we hid, as it were, our faces from Him; He was despised, and we did not esteem Him (Isaiah 53:3).

It seemed the Lord was telling me, "Losing Joseph on earth was part of this verse of Jesus feeling sorrow and grief." However, Jesus had to (and wanted to) submit to the Father's will (John 5:19). He only did what His Father told Him to do. The Father must not have told Him to raise Joseph from the dead. In our case, the Spirit's leading was, "Let go." We did obey, but not at first. This revelation spurs me on to listen more closely to the Spirit so I do not waste time and energy running down paths the Spirit has not led me down. I am ever learning and growing in my walk with the Lord.

Daily Life Now

Mom stayed for about a month, and what a blessing she was. By then, I had physically healed quite a bit. After she went home, Sam and the kids and I drew even closer. Something like this is very trying, and I saw how the Lord was healing us all at different rates. We kept talking about various dreams or things the Lord was showing us. I slowly began to laugh more and cry less, and I kept exercising and losing the pregnancy weight. We picked up the pace with homeschool, and Sam went back to work. The Lord kept healing my heart at an amazing rate, and I kept seeking Him daily. We continued singing His praise in the home and speaking in tongues often.

During this time, the Lord nudged me to start a women's Bible study out of our home, so I did. He also began opening doors for me to encourage other moms who have lost little ones in the womb or right after birth. My compassion for them is very real and deep. All glory to God.

Blessed be the God and Father of our Lord Jesus Christ,
the Father of mercies and God of all comfort, who comforts

us in all our tribulation, that we may be able to comfort
those who are in any trouble, with the comfort with which
we ourselves are comforted by God (2 Corinthians 1:3–4).

My family and I will never stop telling people how good God is and how much He loves each of us. He is good when things are going well, and He is good when things are *not* going well. We often think of James and our other sweet babies in heaven, but our pain is mingled with hope – knowing we will be with them one day in heaven. The separation is only temporary (1 Thessalonians 4:13-18).

God has done a wonderful job healing us inside and out. It's only by God's grace that I'm still standing and smiling today. He put joy in my soul and determination in my heart to love Him forever. There is no real sting in death for the believers because we will all be united someday.

"O Death, where is your sting? O Hades, where is your
victory?" The sting of death is sin, and the strength of sin
is the law. But thanks be to God, who gives us the victory
through our Lord Jesus Christ (1 Corinthians 15:55–57).

Final Thoughts

B y sharing our story, I hope you are encouraged and strengthened. If you are a believer in Jesus, and you feel like you are being squeezed on all sides of life, you're not alone! You are most likely one of God's friends, posing a great threat to the kingdom of darkness. Keep listening to the Father for direction; let Him lead you. And when you've done everything you can do, just keep standing.

> *Therefore take up the whole armor of God, that you may*
> *be able to withstand in the evil day, and having done*
> *all, to stand.* (Ephesians 6:13)

Nuggets to remember that bring healing and joy:

-   Love the Father, and keep trusting Him even when life hurts or crushes you (Matthew 22:37)

-   Keep singing and praising the Father whether you feel like it or not (Hebrews 13:15)

-   If you have received the gift of speaking in tongues, speak in tongues and sing in tongues often (Mark 16:17; 1 Corinthians 14:15)

- Ask the Father to heal your soul from harsh words people may have spoken over you (Matthew 16:19)

- Ask the Father to heal your soul from any trauma you've experienced in your past (Matthew 16:19)

- As the Spirit leads you to, preach the gospel, heal the sick, cleanse the lepers, raise the dead, and cast out demons in Jesus' name (Matthew 10:7–8)

May the Lord be with you always.

> *"For I know the plans I have for you," declares the Lord, "plans to prosper you and not to harm you, plans to give you hope and a future."* (Jeremiah 29:11 NIV)

Prayer for Salvation

I f any of you would like to accept Messiah as your Savior, follow me in this prayer and really mean it in your heart. You must first repent of your sins, your old way of thinking, sinful habits, and so on. You must truly want to change your life to follow the Lord. Once you have repented, then believe by faith that Jesus is Lord and receive His gift of salvation.

"Father, I repent for my sins. Please forgive me and help me to change. Thank you for sending Your Son to die on the cross for my sins. I believe in You. Please come into my life and save me! I invite You to be the Lord of my life."

It is imporant to realize this decision to follow the Lord will likely bring persecution from the enemy. However, remember the Lord will be with you and help you. Hold fast to your confession of faith. Find a Bible, and read it often, from beginning to end. Pray to the Father often and ask Him to give you wisdom while doing your best to obey quickly.

And what is God's "living message"? It is the revelation of faith for salvation, which is the message that we preach. For if you publicly declare with your mouth that Jesus is Lord and believe in your heart that God raised Him from the dead, you will experience salvation.

The heart that believes in Him receives the gift of the righteousness of God -- and then the mouth confesses, resulting in salvation. (Romans 10:9-10)

Prayer to Receive the Baptism
of the Holy Spirit

I f you are a believer in Messiah but have not been baptized with
the power of the Holy Spirit, believe by faith and ask the
Father for it. This power is *dunamis* for miracles, boldness, in
sharing the gospel, amazing love for others, healing, power
over the demonic, and more.

*"Heavenly Father, thank you for sending the power of the Holy
Spirit as a gift to all believers. Please baptize me now in this
power. Help me to walk dynamically on earth like Your Son did
-- loving You and loving others."*

> *For God's promise of the Holy Spirit is for you and*
> *your families, for those yet to be born and for*
> *everyone whom the Lord our God calls to Himself.*
> (Acts 2:39)

From here, study the Scriptures and ask God to help you grow
in the authority He has given you. From my own experience
and that of Scripture, you should notice something right away
(one or more gifts manifesting). Ask the Father to explain the
gifts He has given you. Then, do your best to use them
for God's Kingdom, as He leads you.

You can look at 1 Corinthians 12, 13, and 14 to understand the various gifts, but make sure you love God and love others first (1 Corinthians 13). Love your God with all your heart (Deuteronomy 6:5). Love your neighbors as yourself (Leviticus 19:17-18). From here, the gifts should flow, as He wills.

Remember, it is the same Holy Spirit who distributes, activates, and operates these different gifts as he chooses for each believer. (1 Corinthians 12:11)

Note from Katie:

I have enjoyed our time together. Thank you for joining me. I pray the Scriptures in this book and my life stories have drawn you closer to the Father.

If you are struggling in your walk with the Lord or just need encouragement or someone to speak with about the Lord, please feel free to reach me and my husband by email.

We would be happy to talk with you or pray with you. We can also send you a Bible or try to help you get connected with a local body of believers where you live. You are not alone.

In Him,
Katie Lopez
MyGodWhoNeverFails@gmail.com

References

1. NKJV Bible (all verse unless noted otherwise)

2. Amplified Bible (noted)

3. NIV Bible (noted)

4. The Passion (noted)

5. Little House on the Prairie, Season 1, Episode 13-14, December 18, 1974

6. Dr. Kevin Zadai
   http://www.youtube.com/@KevinZadai

7. Kat Kerr
   a. http://www.youtube.com/ElijahClips (with Kat Kerr)
   b. http://www.revealingheaven.com

8. Robin Bullock
   a. http://www.youtube.com/ElijahClips (with Robin Bullock)
   b. http://www.RobinDBullock.com

9. Smith Wigglesworth
   The Teachings of Smith Wigglesworth by Smith Wigglesworth. Published by Pantianos Classics 1938

10. T.L. Osborn

    Healing the Sick by T.L. Osborn. Published by Harrison House Inc. 1992

11. For King & Country

    "Priceless"Album, Run Wild. Live Free. Love Strong. Released in 2014.

12. The Strongs Concordance

    Strong's #5331: pharmakeia (pronounced far-mak-i'-ah) from 5332

www.ingramcontent.com/pod-product-compliance
Lightning Source LLC
Chambersburg PA
CBHW051621120626
46551CB00014B/1889